PRAISE F

"Timely and well-written, *Wire Your Brain for Confidence* translates complex research into understandable, practical, and vital tools not just for surviving the modern world, but remaking it. Amidst all the competition, demands upon our time, and societal pressure, Louisa Jewell provides a clear path forward for girls and women everywhere striving to define success and worth for themselves."

SHAWN ACHOR, *New York Times* bestselling author of *The Happiness Advantage*

"If you've ever struggled with self-doubt, this book might do you some good. After spending years studying the roots of confidence, Louisa Jewell offers a toolkit for building and rebuilding it."

ADAM GRANT, #1 *New York Times* bestselling author of *Give and Take*, *Originals*, and *Option B* with Sheryl Sandberg

"On our path towards a happier life, there may be no more important journey than the one from self-doubt to self-confidence. In *Wire Your Brain for Confidence*, Louisa Jewell provides an easy-to-use yet well-researched map that you can use for this important journey."

TAL BEN-SHAHAR, *New York Times* bestselling author of *Happier* and *Choose the Life You Want*

"*Wire Your Brain for Confidence* offers a practical step-by-step guide to achieving goals for anyone who has struggled with self-doubt. Louisa Jewell demystifies the science behind action-oriented confidence and makes it accessible to all. This book will empower you to go for your dreams and live your happiest life."

MARCI SHIMOFF, #1 *New York Times* bestselling author of *Happy for No Reason* and *Chicken Soup for the Woman's Soul*

"*Wire Your Brain for Confidence* is a remarkable book for anyone who aspires to have more confidence, success, and overall well-being! Louisa Jewell has written a brilliant book that is steeped in research and filled with novel ideas and memorable stories. I learned things from this book that I will use for years to come."

TOM RATH, #1 *New York Times* bestselling author of *How Full Is Your Bucket?*, *StrengthsFinder 2.0*, *Eat Move Sleep*, and *Are You Fully Charged?*

Wire Your Brain for Confidence

Wire Your Brain

Louisa Jewell, MAPP

for Confidence

The Science of Conquering Self-Doubt

FWP
FAMOUS WARRIOR PRESS

Copyright © 2017 by Louisa Jewell

All rights reserved. No part of this book may be reproduced, stored in a retrieval system or transmitted, in any form or by any means, without the prior written consent of the publisher or a licence from The Canadian Copyright Licensing Agency (Access Copyright). For a copyright licence, visit www.accesscopyright.ca or call toll free to 1-800-893-5777.

Famous Warrior Press
www.louisajewell.com
Toronto ON

ISBN 978-0-9959909-0-6 (paperback)
ISBN 978-0-9959909-1-3 (ebook)

Produced by Page Two
www.pagetwostrategies.com
Cover and interior design by Peter Cocking

To my mother, Bianca,
who ignited a passion in me to improve the lives of all women,
and to my Zia Lina, who believed I could.

Yes, there were times, I'm sure you knew
When I bit off more than I could chew
But through it all, when there was doubt
I ate it up and spit it out
I faced it all and I stood tall
And did it my way

FROM "MY WAY" BY FRANK SINATRA
(LYRICS BY PAUL ANKA)

Contents

Introduction:
Why Women Need to Rule the World 1

1 How Self-Doubt Was Ruining My Life and What I Did about It 8

2 Why Is Everyone Plagued with Self-Doubt, and What Causes It? 22

3 How to Motivate Yourself to Conquer Self-Doubt (Yes, You Can Do It) 44

4 How to Say Yes When Your Brain Is Saying No 72

5 Build Your Confidence Muscles 99

6 What to Do When You Fall 127

7 How to Embrace Failure 151

8 Seeing to Believe 168

9 Surround Yourself with the Right People 186

10 Use Your Body and Emotions as Power 209

Conclusion: Now It's Your Turn 225

Acknowledgments 229

Notes 233

Bibliography 237

Introduction
Why Women Need to Rule the World

• • • • •

IT IS TIME for women to have an equal say at ruling the world. Even if you have no desire to rule the world, just stay with me for a moment.

I am not a man-hater. I love men (maybe too much). I just believe that men and women are different. Women think differently. We have a different social consciousness.

My thinking on this topic began many years ago when I read an article about microloans. These are tiny loans that banks make to people in developing countries to fund new business ventures. Some microfinancers target women exclusively, not only because they have higher repayment rates but also because if you lend a woman money for her business, she is more likely to contribute larger portions of her earnings to the household than a man would. As a result, the children of these female entrepreneurs have a higher likelihood of being enrolled in school full-time, with lower dropout rates. In fact, research shows that these women invest in their children's education first. They also have better health practices and nutrition than other households.[1] Microfinancers discovered that when you invest in female business ventures, you make those women's communities better places to live.

Another important consideration is that if we want to have our needs served and advocate for our children and families, it is much easier to do so from a position of executive power. Here is a simple example: Facebook's chief operating officer, Sheryl Sandberg, in her book *Lean In*, describes her difficult walk from the end of the parking lot at Google (where she was working at the time) when she was uncomfortably pregnant. She complained to Larry Page and Sergey Brin, Google cofounders, who shortly afterward created parking spots for pregnant women close to the office building.[2] But Sandberg had not thought of this consideration until she actually went through the experience of being pregnant herself, and she wouldn't have been able to influence such a swift change if she hadn't been in the senior position she was. Now imagine women having an equal voice in all decisions from a position of executive leadership and you can see how much easier it would be to influence policy and meet the needs of more and more women in the world, on matters more important than a front-row parking spot. Imagine the shifts we could see if women populated 50 percent of every leadership rank in government, academia, and corporations.

This shift becomes even more critical when you think about the incredible influence corporations have on government policy. We have seen time and time again how government policies that are not helpful for our populations at large continue to get approved. Corporate dollars act as significant lobbying power that can be used every day to influence government decisions. If enough pressure is placed on certain politicians in power, those politicians can sway the direction of government policy. The problem is that women occupy a small percentage of executive positions.[3] As of 2016, women held only 32.1 percent of senior management roles, and there was only one woman head on the TSX 60. A recent Conference Board of Canada study cites many reasons for this low level of representation of women at senior levels, including the fact that women have to navigate a more complex career structure because of family responsibilities and discomfort with self-promotion.[4] The study also highlights that women in positions of power often lack the support they need and thus, when they fail, it is blamed on their gender rather than a lack of support. Negative gender stereotyping is another obstacle women must deal with regularly. This means women have a lot more challenges to overcome while trying to rise to the top than men do.

The 2015 Women's Leadership Study, commissioned by American Express and Women of Influence, found that only 32 percent of women believe that gaining executive-level jobs is achievable, and less than 28 percent aspire to it.[5] That's because women in the study felt that "loving what I do" was more important than climbing the corporate ladder. In fact, 17 percent of these women stated they had turned down promotions because the job was not a good fit. In general, women are ambitious, but they also want to stay true to their values and achieve work-life balance.

Many of the women I know left their corporate jobs to start their own businesses because they wanted to fashion a life for themselves that was more meaningful, engage in the work they love, and have more control over their daily lives. That was certainly true for me. I always say that I am completely unemployable and could never work for anyone else again. But many women I know struggle to earn the income required for a sustainable business. I certainly struggled for many years before my business was financially sustainable. Some highly successful women I know even feel shame when they achieve high levels of income, feeling that if they are "doing it for the money," they must be a bad person. In my lifetime I have heard many men celebrate and brag about their 100K/month milestones, but never have I heard a man express shame over it. Even when we are successful, we are doubting ourselves.

I have the privilege and honor to be friends, colleagues, and associates with thousands of women who are doing amazing work. I am also witness to their never-ending struggle to feel good enough. I know too many successful and accomplished women who still go home at the end of each day and question their every move. Women who have risen through the ranks, done the work, and have many university degrees are still questioning if they are good enough. There is something really wrong with this.

This book is for those of you who feel this way. This book is not about building general confidence; I know you have lots of that. It's about building the kind of confidence that leaves you unwavering in your belief in yourself and the life you want to live. It's about not questioning yourself all the time and moving

Sometimes the smallest step in the right direction ends up being the biggest step of your life. Tiptoe if you must, but take a step.

NAEEM CALLAWAY

forward with enthusiasm. It's about finding that peaceful calm and letting go of anxiety and stress. It's for those of you who are playing a bigger game and want to do it with greater joy every day.

I want to help you overcome any obstacle with self-assuredness and rise to the top, because if we have more women at the top, the world will benefit. I want you to go after everything you want *because you want it*, not because it's someone else's idea of success. And I want you to do it while feeling in control, calm, balanced, and happy. After all, what is the purpose of success if you are feeling overwhelmed, stressed out, unfulfilled, and unhappy?

If you want to live an authentic life, you need the courage to defend your unique definition of success. Whether that is being a stay-at-home mom, working for yourself, or working for someone else, you want to feel good about your life. If you are in business, you want to do what you love and make enough money doing it to sustain the life you want and deserve, for yourself and your family. You don't want to just survive, you want to thrive. I call this feeling—being successful but also healthy and happy—*flourishing*. The secret of reaching this flourishing state is to overcome self-doubt and build your confidence.

Flourishing requires confidence to stand up and go after what you want, to persevere in the face of setbacks and criticism. It requires the confidence to believe that success is on its way. It requires the confidence to care less about what people think, so that you can continue to forge a new path.

I do not profess to be the most confident person in the world. I believe that achieving confidence is not a one-time thing. As you go after a bigger life, your confidence will be challenged. You will (and I do) have moments of doubt, which, I will show you, are not necessarily negative. This book is about conquering and mastering your self-doubt. You know that moment when you want to put your hand up and say "Yes! I want to do that!" but your body and your brain stop you? You know those times when you want to speak up, make that call, send that email, invite that person out on a date, or say no to a pushy colleague, but you just can't muster the confidence? This book is all about the science behind what it takes to wire your brain for *Yes, I will do it.*

This book is about confidence, but more specifically it is about the related concept of self-efficacy. Self-efficacy is what gives you the *courage to act*, that defining moment when you know you want to say yes but you are stopping yourself. It is specific to certain situations, like asking someone to dance. I believe that success comes not with one big yes but with hundreds of smaller yeses along the way. This book explores what influences our behavior at the moment that moves us away from or toward our dreams. By deciphering the science behind your ability to act, you might better understand your behavior and navigate your way to success more effectively.

I have gathered scientific tools and methods for finding the courage to say yes to the life you really want. These tools and exercises are rooted in psychology, the latest research in neuroscience, and the science of our mind-body connection. They've also worked for me, and I continue to practice them in my work and personal life. Through numerous examples and case studies, I will show you how it's possible to go after what you desire—whatever that is—so you can live your most vibrant life.

The life you deserve.

1

How Self-Doubt Was Ruining My Life and What I Did about It

• • • • •

I DISCOVERED MY SELF-DOUBT in a very unlikely way.

When I was seventeen years old, I was one of the head cheerleaders at Stephen Leacock Collegiate in Toronto, Canada. Our team decided to enter the All-Ontario Cheerleading Championships for the first time. In fact, it was the first cheerleading competition the school had *ever* entered. I have to say that we were much more interested in hanging out with the boys on the football team than we were in actually cheering, but we thought competing would be fun. The problem was that our team was nowhere near the caliber of other competing teams. We were much smaller than other teams, with only nine tiny girls on the squad, and we did not have even one person on our team who could carry, throw, or bear heavy loads. We also didn't have anyone who could do gymnastics, so our routines were pretty unsophisticated.

In a nutshell, we were bad.

So we knew we wouldn't win the competition on talent. We would need a strategy. We decided that our core strategy was to win by showing the judges that we were the team with the *most spirit*—after all, isn't that what cheerleading is all about? So we set a plan in motion to show our love for our school at every opportunity.

I had all the girls on our team collect jerseys from our other sports teams, so we would always be wearing something that bore the name Stephen Leacock. We were staying at a hotel for three days during the competition, and we wanted to make sure that the judges, staying at the same hotel, knew who Stephen Leacock was. Wherever we went, we were dressed the same, and we cheered "Thank you!" to our waiters, "Good-bye!" to the concierge, and "Have a good day!" to the doorman. Everywhere we went we cheered "Leacock, Leacock, Leacock!" (By the time the competition was over, I had lost my voice completely.) The guys on the football team actually came to cheer *us* on. We delivered our competing routine and were surprised that we did well enough to make it to the final round.

At the end of the competition, all fifty teams were called into the hotel's ballroom for the announcement of the winners. "We decided we would name the top four teams instead of the top three because there were just so many great teams this year," the announcer said. I thought the judges must have done that in order to honor us because we showed a lot of spirit but were lacking technically. How thoughtful of them.

They called the fourth-place team—not us—and that team exploded into ecstatic screams and soared into the air. *Aha*, I thought, *so I wonder*... Then the judges called third place—again, not us. Uproarious cheers from that team. At this point, my optimism waned. I knew we were not good enough to be in first or second place, so I looked around the room and wondered who it could be. Laurier had some great dance routines, but Woburn was good too. Then the judges called the team that had won second place—again, not us. I thought, *Oh good, they deserved it.* I scanned the room of fifty teams but couldn't put my finger on the winner. Finally, the announcement...

"And the winner of the All-Ontario Cheerleading Championships, beating out forty-nine teams in Ontario, is... STEPHEN LEACOCK COLLEGIATE." In an instant, all of us exploded out of our seats into a frenzy of screaming, leaping, and crying. We were shocked and elated. Then the announcer said, "Congratulations to Stephen Leacock Collegiate. The judges chose you as the winners because you are the team that showed the most spirit—and after all, isn't that what cheerleading is all about?"

I was stunned. The announcer had repeated our own exact words, the core of our winning strategy. We had known our weaknesses, we were aware of our strengths, and we knew exactly what the judges would find most desirable. We'd hit the nail right on the head. We had a vision, we were creative in our approach, and we flawlessly executed that vision.

I was a leader on this team. So why had I been looking around the room absolutely convinced we could not be the champions? Not only was I not even hopeful—I was *positive* we wouldn't win. I had no faith in my own strategy. I had given up and written myself off, along with my whole team. How could I have been so out of touch with reality?

Later I realized that this level of self-doubt affected my emotional state throughout the competition. I was a wreck, making us practice over and over again until we were perfect. I was exhausted and the team was exhausted before we even got to the competition. After the competition I didn't believe I was a better leader—I thought that our win was based either on luck or the abilities of the other cheerleaders on my team.

That experience revealed something so fundamentally puzzling not only about myself but about human behavior: *my thoughts and beliefs about myself and my capabilities could be very different from the reality of the situation, regardless of feedback, evidence, and experience.* This revelation had such a profound effect on me, and yet all I could think was "What is wrong with me?" I didn't yet have the tools and knowledge to do something to change this for myself.

Can you relate to this story? Have you achieved a certain level of success and yet you still go home every night questioning yourself and your decisions? Do you overthink when things go wrong and focus on your "mistakes"? Are you exhausted from never feeling good enough or not being perfect? Do you put enormous effort into things you have done time and time again because you are worried you are going to fail? Are you wondering why your thoughts are so different from your reality?

You may be suffering from chronic self-doubt.

Self-Doubt Was Ruining My Life

As I got older, I realized the impact self-doubt was having on my life. First of all, it robbed me of my happiness. I was a high achiever, but I always doubted I was good enough. I felt that I hadn't done enough, I wasn't making enough money, I wasn't popular enough, I wasn't skinny enough, I wasn't a good enough mother, my home wasn't nice enough, the car I drove was not fancy enough, and I surely didn't think anyone would be interested in what I had to say. Looking around at colleagues who were accomplishing more and making more money just confirmed that I didn't have the talent to be successful. Often I asked myself, *What is wrong with me? Why haven't I achieved the level of success of so and so?* Every time I tried something new, I was so stressed out and worked an exorbitant number of hours because I doubted whether I could do a good job. Even when I received positive feedback I doubted it was because of my actions but rather figured it was because of some amazing stroke of luck. I was miserable.

The problem with self-doubters is that often the image they have created in their own heads is far from what others see. From the outside looking in, I was pretty successful. I'd completed my degree in business at the University of Toronto and landed a great job at IBM. I married a lovely man, and had a nice home in a great neighborhood and two beautiful daughters. But I was never able to enjoy my success because I felt like a failure and an impostor. There is no gray zone for chronic self-doubters: you are either a huge success or a complete failure.

My self-doubt also stopped me from going after my big dream. I didn't believe I had the capability, talent, or experience to be a professional speaker and writer. I wanted to inspire and help others. I wanted to travel the world. I wanted to create an organization and grow it. I did not feel talented enough to do any of that. I was too anxious to even think about it. I would see others doing it and think, *I want to do that.* I would dream about it every day, and the dreams made me feel wonderful. But as soon as I thought about taking any steps toward turning those dreams into a reality, I became too scared to actually do anything. So my dreams remained just that—dreams.

Self-doubt also showed up as repetitive negative thinking, what psychologists call rumination. I questioned decisions I'd made, I'd get overly upset about casual comments people made to me, I wondered if I was dressed properly for the occasion, I stressed about emails... you name it, I was ruminating about it. My ruminations paralyzed me from going after my big dreams. After small setbacks, my ruminations would be so pervasive I would picture harming myself. Even when I had some success, I would quickly engage in self-sabotaging behavior, never believing I could recreate that success.

My self-doubt was affecting my mental health. Research shows that chronic second-guessing can lead to depression, anxiety, and mood swings. In five studies involving over seven hundred college students, principal investigator and Ohio State University psychology professor Herbert Mirels and researchers Paul Greblo and Janet Dean found that self-doubters, compared with their more confident peers, had lower self-esteem and higher degrees of anxiety, depression, and procrastination.[6] The researchers concluded that self-doubters might be more prone to depression because they often feel their life is out of their control. That is exactly where self-doubt led me.

My Battle with Depression

About eighteen years ago, I went through some hardships that separated me from my family of origin and created a lot of sadness for me. At the same time, I was pregnant with my second child. At nine weeks, while my husband, Tim, and I were out enjoying dinner at our favorite restaurant, I began to feel severe cramps. They came on so fast and hard, I didn't know what was going on. I ran to the bathroom, to find that I was bleeding profusely. I knew I had lost my baby. I couldn't believe that I was in a restaurant bathroom while all our hopes and dreams had just shattered. I was distraught and in shock. I ran out of the bathroom and told my husband that we had to go. Not questioning, Tim threw money down on the table and we ran out. I collapsed in his arms in the street and told him what had happened. We held each other tightly as we both cried for the loss of our precious child. We were devastated.

That would not be the end of it. That year, I would miscarry another three times. Miscarrying is like a roller-coaster ride—you are thrilled and elated to be pregnant, and then you come crashing down with great speed. After each miscarriage, I lost more and more hope. Shortly after my fourth miscarriage, I fell into a deep and dark depression.

My days were consumed with anger. My mind was a hamster wheel of ruminations. If you have ever had depression, you know that it paralyzes you from engaging in your life. No one else seems to understand why you're not capable of doing a stitch of housework or why you're still in pajamas at four in the afternoon. With depression, you look absolutely fine to everyone, not obviously ill, and they wonder why you just can't snap out of it. At every turn, my internal voices reminded me that I was not smart enough, rich enough, accomplished enough, or worthy enough of love or success. *I was not enough.*

No matter what I did, those voices interrupted every opportunity I had for happiness.

At school, they teach you how to do math and make grilled-cheese sandwiches, but nobody teaches Happiness 101. Doesn't happiness seem like an important subject? Day after day, I lay around the house. Even simple things like taking my daughter to the park were very difficult for me. I was numb, and I didn't know what to do to get out of it.

One afternoon I was in my pajamas, watching a local talk show. A psychologist was being interviewed. And it dawned on me: there are people out there who can help!

So I set up an appointment to see this psychologist, and you know what he taught me?

I had some very screwed-up ways of thinking.

Thank you. That's good to know.

He would listen to my stories and say things like, "You know, Louisa, people who love each other don't tell each other to fuck off." And I was like, "Really?" I'm Sicilian, so that was news to me!

After many meetings with him, I realized that he was challenging my way of thinking. I discovered that my problems were not the source of my depression. *My way of thinking* was the source of my depression. The way I framed situations in my life made a difference between whether I was angry or accepting. Every time I went to his office, I felt better. I was coping better. My ruminations were not so all-consuming. I was able to engage with my daughter again. Thankfully, I got pregnant again and carried my sweet second daughter to full term. I was getting out of the house every day. I felt like my life was back in my control. When I thought I was feeling good enough, I stopped going to therapy.

But six months later, something would trigger feelings of depression again. I would find myself unable to get out of bed and unable to engage in life, and I would spiral downward. Once again, I'd find myself in my therapist's office. After going back and forth, I finally decided that I had to understand what it was he was doing to help me think in healthier ways. I needed to know what he knew.

So I decided to educate myself about happiness and psychological well-being. I discovered that there is a whole scientific study of psychological well-being called "positive psychology." I spent a year pursuing my master's degree in applied positive psychology (MAPP) at the University of Pennsylvania. I studied with the field's founding father, internationally renowned psychologist and researcher Dr. Martin "Marty" Seligman. I also studied with other prominent positive psychologists—Dr. Chris Peterson, Dr. Barbara Fredrickson, Dr. Roy Baumeister,

Your worst enemy cannot harm you as much as your own unguarded thoughts.

BUDDHA

and Dr. David Cooperrider, to name a few. I read over six thousand pages of academic research, and I applied everything I learned to myself. The knowledge I gained transformed my life, and so far I have not fallen back into depression—not even close. *Wow,* I wondered, *why doesn't everyone know about this?*

As I learned more about positive psychology, I discovered it is not only about happiness. It was about how to be psychologically strong, how to reach higher levels of performance, how to be resilient in the face of extreme challenges. I learned how to persevere and how to bounce back from failure. I learned how to self-regulate, which has helped me stick to my diet and exercise routines. I learned how to manage my daily moods and maintain a positive mental energy so that I can be productive all day. I learned how to be more compassionate to others and to myself. I also became more peaceful. The voices in my head were silenced. I mean, completely. Can you imagine not having those negative voices in your head? But one day it just happened. *Absolute silence.* I was free at last.

All this knowledge allowed me to conquer my chronic self-doubt, and once I did, I thrived! I wasn't afraid of going after my big dreams anymore. I went after everything I wanted, without feelings of failure or constant negative ruminations. I stopped self-sabotaging, and I engaged in difficult challenges. I realized my dream of becoming a speaker and a writer. I now speak to audiences around the world. I teach at two universities, run workshops for hundreds of clients across North America every year, and speak at several conferences annually. My work focuses on inspiring and helping others.

I founded the Canadian Positive Psychology Association (CPPA) in 2012 with a handful of dedicated colleagues whom I had recruited, and it is growing every year. The CPPA's mission is to disseminate the research and applications in positive psychology to all Canadians, to improve their mental well-being and promote positive mental health. We run conferences every year, drawing speakers and delegates from all over the world. I want everyone to have this knowledge. What I do all day, every day, is teach people how to live a more vibrant life, and I love every second of it.

I feel so blessed and joyful to be living the life I always wanted for myself. I still get fearful sometimes, but I have the mental tools to deal with that fear. When I do have moments of self-doubt—which is totally normal and healthy, as I will soon explain—I am no longer filled with stress and anxiety. I know how to manage the feeling and use it to flourish.

As I achieve higher goals, I have peace of mind—a quiet confidence. I now live a bigger life, yet I am calm, and I trust in my abilities as I go about my business. I cannot even begin to describe the difference it has made in my life to conquer my self-doubt. I knew once I had discovered all this great knowledge and these scientific findings that I had to share them with others.

Even though I have become a more positive version of myself, life has still thrown me some curveballs; it's how I respond that is most important. In 2014, my husband of nineteen years left me and we began divorce proceedings. Although we have an amicable relationship, the sadness and the impact on my family was overwhelming. At around the same time, my mother, who was eighty-eight and living in a retirement home, decided to stop eating. We tried every possible thing to get her to engage in life again but, sadly, nine months later she died. Watching her deteriorate the way she did was at times too much to bear. Six weeks after that, my beloved father-in-law died after a four-year battle with Parkinson's disease. I often say 2015 was the most challenging year of my life. But this time around, I was grateful I had so many tools to keep myself healthy and happy despite the events. It was this knowledge that kept me strong and continuing to persevere toward my goals, including writing this book.

I wrote this book for my younger, cheerleading self and for all of you with chronic self-doubt. It's time for you to become the person you really want to be, courageous enough to create the life you really want. I wrote this book for those of you reaching for higher heights and playing a bigger game but feeling that every day is just an upward battle. I hope the knowledge you gain by reading this book will help you set a new trajectory for your life.

Psychologists and researchers know exactly what it takes to change inhibiting behaviors to those that will motivate you to go after your most desired goals. They know how you can be fearful and act anyway. Now you will have this knowledge, plus strategies for not just reducing self-doubt but also building positive psychological resources and confidence.

I have acquired deep knowledge on this topic, but I am still learning and growing every day. Confidence is not something you build once and then it's there forever. Confidence is like a muscle: you need to be practicing confidence-building habits every day to keep that muscle strong. This book will teach you those techniques and the science behind them.

The information in this book is based on scientific evidence and research. I have met many researchers and academics who are doing brilliant work, but many of them don't stop to consider how to apply their research to helping people solve problems. That is what I do: I create a bridge between the ivory tower and main street. I take complex scientific findings and translate them into easy-to-use, practical tools so anyone new to the topic can easily absorb them. Each chapter equips you with the knowledge you need to understand the science in easy terms, using stories from everyday people like you and me. Each chapter includes practical exercises that you can incorporate into your daily life.

No matter where you are in your life, no matter what you want or how far away you are from getting it, I hope you will use these tools to live a happier, more fulfilling life. Building confidence is about a new way of being. Once you discover the freedom that comes with confidence, you will feel empowered to go after whatever it is you want—and flourish!

2

Why Is Everyone Plagued with Self-Doubt, and What Causes It?

A LOT OF PEOPLE were curious why such a positive person like me would write a book about self-doubt. I have explained how destructive it was to me personally, but I also know that chronic self-doubt prevents us from following our heart and crafting our authentic life. Mastering self-assuredness comes first with an understanding of how the opposite—self-doubt—can destroy your motivation for creating the life you want and deserve. Doubting your abilities can kill your motivation and block you entirely from moving toward your goals. I knew I was plagued by self-doubt, but I had no understanding of where it came from. What causes it? How does it affect my courage to act? I was curious to have the answers so I could better understand myself. I wanted to know why I would easily say yes to some things, even very difficult things, and then feel immobilized with fear when it came to other things. Especially things I really wanted to do! Every day, scientists discover ways to understand human behavior, so that we may navigate life with greater ease. When I first embarked on the study of self-doubt, I learned about the Laboratory on the Uncertain Self at Ohio State University. Yes, a whole group of people have dedicated their lives to the study of self-doubt! They have contributed a great deal to my understanding.

Why Are So Many of Us Plagued by Self-Doubt?

Self-doubt is defined as "a general sense of feeling unsure about one's competencies, abilities, and thus outcomes in daily life that stem from those abilities."[7] Often, low self-esteem is equated with self-doubt, but I want to make a clear distinction between the two. Self-esteem is a person's overall subjective evaluation of his or her self-worth, which is different from our evaluations about how capable we are. Self-doubt is a questioning of our abilities. The two are related because the deeper the self-doubt, the worse we feel about ourselves.

Everywhere I went and spoke about the topic of self-doubt, many people responded with a resounding "Oh yes, that's me!" I wondered what it was about our modern society that has us all plagued with self-doubt. So I interviewed Dr. Patrick Carroll, assistant professor of psychology at Ohio State University at Lima and faculty member at the Laboratory on the Uncertain Self. Dr. Carroll told me, "The first reason is that our social world has become increasingly complex and fluid. If you asked someone who lived four hundred years ago about what they were going to do with their lives, they would probably look at you perplexed. People generally lived in the same place, did the same thing, and were surrounded by the same people their whole lives. Change was a rare occurrence. Fast-forward four hundred years and you will find that change is the only constant in our lives."

Today's world is fast-paced, complex, and ever-changing. We often have to switch projects or careers, move to a new city, learn new online systems, navigate new social media tools, and more. Even if you have a stable job, you're not sure if your company will downsize, right-size, or move in a new direction on any given day. Rich Feller, past president of the National Career Development Association, said in a 2014 keynote, "You are either a business owner or a temp."[8] None of us lives with 100 percent job security. There are so many factors that are out of our control on a daily basis, which makes it more difficult to manage our thoughts and emotions about everything that is going on in our lives.

One of the amazing things about human beings that allowed us to survive and evolve for thousands of years is our incredible ability to adapt and change, which is hardwired into our brain. The brain has many parts, but I want to highlight only two: our older "emotional" or limbic brain, and our newer, more "rational" brain, the neocortex. Psychologists have known for decades that negative emotions played a critical role in our evolutionary survival. As cavepeople, if we suddenly encountered a saber-toothed tiger, negative emotions would trigger many physiological changes in our body that prepared us to either fight or flee. We still have those ancient, "emotional" structures in our brain. Thus, when we encounter threats to our survival, like almost being hit by a car or being robbed at gunpoint, this part of our brain is triggered and prepares us to survive the threat. The problem is that we also go into a fight-or-flight response for purely psychological reasons. Scientists have discovered many common situations that can trigger this stress response. One is uncertainty.

Depending on its complexity or significance, a change feels uncomfortable because it makes things uncertain. The emotional side of our brain is always interested in survival, so our brain craves control and mastery over our environment. We always want to know we can manage. A change may suddenly trigger feelings of uncertainty if we are not sure how it will affect our ability to cope. And these feelings of uncertainty may trigger a stress response, which is processed in the emotional part of our brain. When that emotional part is agitated, it can take over any rational response we may have, making it more difficult for us to engage in executive functioning. All this might be going on subconsciously; we may have general feelings of anxiety or stress and not know why. Intellectually, we may want to move forward, but our emotional brain stops us.

Thus, when new conditions arise, it is natural for our confidence levels to drop and for us to question our abilities. Our brain always wants to know that we can navigate our world effectively, but with all this constant change, we are never sure of that. "This greater certainty of change may ultimately translate into greater uncertainty in self as people struggle to maintain a stable identity in an increasingly unstable world," says Dr. Carroll. "Ironically, then, self-uncertainty or doubt may be one of the few certainties left in modern life." In other words, according to Dr. Carroll, self-doubt may be a normal part of our daily existence in an ever-changing world.[9] If that is the case, we should not expect to eliminate self-doubt from our lives but learn to manage and conquer it. We need new tools so that we can quiet the emotional part of our brain and engage in the more rational thinking required to reach our goals, whatever they may be.

As our environment changes, we could also start to question who we are or who we "should" be. In the late 1990s, I was the director of education for Wired Woman, an organization that encouraged women to pursue careers in technology. At one event, while setting up a meeting with a potential sponsor, I pulled out my paper agenda. The potential sponsor looked at me with disdain and said, "Really, Louisa? Where's your PalmPilot?" (PalmPilots as the personal electronic device of choice were all the rage back then.) Embarrassed, I ran out the next day and purchased one. Suddenly I was not "good enough" without my gadget. When things are changing every day, it's challenging to keep up.

According to Dr. Carroll, another reason we are often plagued with self-doubt concerns our feelings about our own self-competence. From an early age, we receive strong messages that our value in life depends on demonstrating competence and using it to achieve important performance goals. We are a society that measures success by achievements. At parties, the first question we ask is not who are you as a person but "What do you do for a living?" Thus, the question of self-value is linked with the question of whether we feel we are *accomplishing* enough.

After reading a controversial study conducted by Betsey Stevens and Justin Wolfers at the Wharton School of the University of Pennsylvania, titled *The Paradox of Declining Female Happiness*, I had further insight into why self-doubt seemed to affect more women than men. According to the study, women's happiness levels have been declining since the 1970s. They suggest that one of the reasons for this decline is that women, especially younger women, are intensifying the importance of too many domains in their lives:

> The most striking point is that young women are increasingly attaching greater importance to thirteen of the fourteen domains examined... In particular, there appears to be increasing ambition of young women beyond the domestic sphere, with greater importance attached to "being successful in my line of work", "being able to find steady work", "making a contribution to society", and "being a leader in my community". These data arguably suggest that women's life satisfaction may have become more complicated as the women have increased the number of domains in which they wish to succeed. Moreover, these data point to rising pressures beyond the much-discussed work-family tradeoff."[10]

How is it conceivable for women to feel successful when it is almost impossible to excel at thirteen out of fourteen domains?

Somehow we are socialized to believe that we can be *excellent* at every domain in our lives or that we somehow "should" be excellent at every domain. Of course, we never feel that we are good enough because once again, we are holding ourselves to an impossible standard.

Over the years, women's responsibilities have been changing, offering us many more socially accepted roles in society. My mother had one domain in life that she focused on: taking care of her family. In this realm, she cooked, cleaned, helped us kids with homework, took care of us amazingly well, and also took care of my father. She was a big part of her church community, where she volunteered, but nothing interfered with her family duties. Imagine yourself like my mother, caring deeply about home and family.

Now imagine adding another twelve or thirteen domains to your attention span and placing high importance on each domain. I don't know who the first woman was to think we needed to do this, but I think we should hunt her down! It stresses me out just thinking about it, and yet we place this level of importance on these domains every day. Self-doubt is an obvious outcome when we compare ourselves to the highest standard in each of these domains and never feel that we measure up. We want to be top of our game at work, in a loving relationship, the best mom in the world, as good an entertainer as Martha Stewart, head of the school PTA, activists in our communities, Jenna Jameson in the bedroom, a supportive girlfriend, a dog walker, a business owner, an author, and a faithful volunteer.

A beautiful thing is never perfect.

ANONYMOUS

Nowadays, women want to be excellent at everything. Correction: women want to be *perfect* at everything. And when we are not, we feel as if we are failing. I interviewed Alice Domar, PhD, executive director of the Domar Center for Mind/Body Health. Dr. Domar is a leading expert on women and stress. She agreed that women stress about being perfect in all aspects of their lives, and added emphatically, "Whatever the list is, add 'thin' to that too."

Our obsession with looking good is so pervasive, I can't go five minutes online or watching TV without getting some message or other that there is something seriously wrong with me if I don't look twenty-four at the age of fifty, or if I have wrinkles, fat in the "wrong" places, or dark spots on my face. According to a 2009 National Eating Disorders Association press release, "In 1965, the average fashion model weighed just eight percent less than the average American woman... The average fashion model today is 5′11″ and weighs 117 pounds, which makes her thinner than 98 percent of women."[11] Not only do media messages add pressure for women to be thin, but now we are comparing ourselves to an almost impossible standard and feeling like failures.

It is one thing to stress about being perfect if you have only one domain in life that matters; it is quite another to expect to be perfect in fourteen domains! What an impossible burden, bringing with it anxiety, depression, and chronic stress. It is no surprise that approximately 25 percent of North American women are on antidepressants.[12] There aren't enough hours in the day to be perfect in so many areas of our lives.

What Causes Self-Doubt?

Some research indicates that self-doubt may stem from early childhood experiences. According to Dr. Carroll, children who received mixed messages from their parents regarding what they have done well and what earns praise may develop feelings of self-doubt later in life; for example, if parents were inconsistent with their feedback and children were not confident about what garnered praise one day and what garnered criticism the next. Self-doubt is socially constructed, meaning that we highly value what others think about us. We are especially sensitive to messages from our parents, as we have a desire to please them.

Dr. Carroll has also learned that self-doubt can arise because of our interpretation of difficulties when we embark on challenging goals. It is natural for anyone who is starting something new to encounter difficulties. But for some of us, experiencing difficulties in general is a sign that perhaps we are not talented enough or not suited to the endeavor.

For example, many years ago when I was in university, a friend invited me along to watch her dance class. I watched from the open door as a hunky young man led the large group of mainly women, all clad in leotards and leg warmers, in an exhilarating ninety-minute class. Everyone moving in sync—it was amazing to watch. The music, the moves, the energy were all intoxicating. I signed up right away. The fee was more than I could afford for the three-month period, but I was excited to be part of the class. I'd always considered myself a good dancer.

The following night, I arrived in my favorite spandex one-piece (it was the '90s, after all), ready to rock it out. The dashing young instructor entered the room, music blaring, and began: "Five, six, seven, eight!"

He was at the front of the class, demonstrating the moves, the class moving along with him. I made an attempt to keep up but I was a total spaz, stumbling about, and had no clue what I was doing. I banged into the people next to me, who gave me dirty looks, as if to say, "What are *you* doing here?" It was a humiliating ninety minutes. Do you remember the old *Flintstones* cartoons in which Fred, when he was thoroughly embarrassed, would shrink to the size of a mouse and go running out of the room, crying? That is what I felt like doing. I never wanted to go back.

But I had paid a huge amount of money—I *had* to go back! So, at the next class, I found a spot at the very back and in the corner, practically out the door. In walked the instructor, the music started, and voilà... he began the exact same routine. Aha! I realized that everyone else moved so easily as he demonstrated because they all knew the routine. Night after night, it was the same routine. It's not that I was not a talented dancer, I just didn't know the steps. Once I learned, I became good at it. Then I thoroughly enjoyed it. Before long, the instructor was calling me to the front to perform for the others. The point is, it took courage to suck up my embarrassment of the first class and get back into the game. And I am glad I found that courage, because becoming a better dancer brought me tremendous joy. That young man was George Randolph of the Randolph Academy, and I danced with him for five years. I loved every moment of it. Many years later, my daughters went on to dance at the Randolph Academy too.

You will never know if you can be good at something if you don't give it a real go. And by "a real go," I mean spending time building your abilities. Stop focusing on what you look like while you stumble about learning, and focus on *what* you are learning. Dr. Carroll reminds us that many of us are never conditioned to believe that difficulties and stumbling come at the beginning of anything that requires hard work. Let the stumbling at the beginning just be a sign that you haven't worked hard enough yet through the beginning phases. Anything worthwhile is worth struggling through—it should not be perceived as self-doubt or a personal failing, but as a normal part of starting anything new.

Can Self-Doubt Ever Be Helpful?

I know what I am about to say may sound contradictory, given what I've said about the negative consequences of self-doubt, but here goes: having some self-doubt is not necessarily a bad thing. We need to know when self-doubt is useful and when it is not. Once again, I turned to Dr. Carroll for his guidance on this question. He explained that if you are experiencing feelings of self-doubt as you embark on something new, or if you find something very challenging, that is normal and helpful. This feeling might propel you to work harder, seek some much-needed advice, or practice more. These are all steps that will only improve your abilities and ultimately your confidence in that domain. Research confirms that a little self-doubt motivates you to learn more about what you are embarking on.

Your emotions related to doubting yourself give you a clue about how much work you still have to do to complete a task well. Your feelings of confidence give you an idea of how competent you are. Imagine that you are stressed about an upcoming presentation. If you are feeling anxious as a result of your self-doubt, maybe this is a sign that you need to practice more or put more work into it. In this case, self-doubt can be a good thing because it protects you from making a fool of yourself.

Thus, when we have no self-doubt, we could be putting ourselves in jeopardy or possibly putting our careers and reputation on the line. If we never listen to that voice that says, "Wait a second, are you sure you have thought this through or put the required work in?" then we are not paying attention to our own wisdom. If you are embarking on something new, those feelings of low confidence and doubt should propel you to act—which means compel you to practice, seek advice, and work hard. Remember, low confidence does not mean you are not talented; it may mean you have just not worked hard enough.

When Is Self-Doubt Not Helpful?

So how do we know when to trust those internal voices of self-doubt or when to tell them to shut up? To understand when self-doubt is not helpful or when it is chronic, ask yourself if any of the following statements are true:

1. I often question my abilities across many domains of my life (e.g., at work, at home, in social situations, on the tennis court).

2. Even though I have performed a certain task many times, I still spend an enormous amount of time completing it, because I want to make sure it is good enough and, in the end, I still may feel it is not good enough.

3. When I embark on an important endeavor, I spend more time worrying about failing than I do feeling good about the task at hand.

4. When I embark on an important task, I try to think of every possible thing that could go wrong, and then I spend a great deal of time engaging in contingencies to prepare for any situation that may arise.

5. I spend a lot of time questioning if I can succeed at important activities in my life.

6. I put a lot of effort into avoiding failure, because this brings me a sense of relief.

7. Even when I get good results after completing a task, I often attribute the successful outcome to other colleagues, my team, or a stroke of good fortune, rather than to my efforts or skills.

8. Even when things go well, at the end of the day, I question whether I did things right, or I focus primarily on the few things that went wrong.

If you answered yes to two or more of these statements, you may be suffering from chronic self-doubt. These questions are a good measure of how obsessed you are with your uncertainty about your capabilities. Researchers have found that those with chronic self-doubt spend less time positively focused on the task at hand and more time and energy focused on avoiding or planning to avoid failure. When you are thinking about going after a bigger goal in your life or a new challenge, are you mainly preoccupied with what can go wrong? If you are heavily focused on the negative, you cannot joyfully engage in your goal pursuits. When I first started designing workshops, I was so filled with self-doubt that I focused all my energy on not screwing up. I had so much anxiety, I gave myself ulcers! So if you answered yes to two or more of these statements, your focus may not be productive and will detract from your courage to act.

Chronic self-doubt has consequences: it can stop you from asking for a promotion even when you are a star at work; it can stop you from contacting people to get more business even when you have a fabulous product to sell; and it may stop you from asking that cute guy or gal out for a date even though they make small talk with you every day. When you have chronic self-doubt, your life is constantly filled with hesitation, resistance, and anxiety.

Or maybe you have become quite competent at a certain task but you continue to hesitate. One simple clue might be when many people praise you for your good work but you constantly doubt their praise. Maybe you have garnered the respect of your peers, and you continually progress and succeed—and external markers, like a corner office, promotion, or salary increase, make this clear—and yet you go home every night questioning your performance. Or perhaps you don't offer to take on that prestigious project, even when you know you would be great at it. It's self-doubt that is holding you back.

If you are filled with self-doubt about every action you take, you will be paralyzed, anxious, and ineffective—not to mention miserable! If you are so fearful of failure, disappointment, or putting yourself out there that you can't take even one step toward your goals, you may look back on your life with regret. You know you are capable of a bigger life, but those voices in your head act as the roadblock.

Are you stopping yourself from going after what you really want because you constantly feel you are not smart, talented, or pretty enough? If that's the case, you need to tackle your self-doubt. The good news is that you've taken the first step: you are reading this book!

Your next step is to...

Eliminate Perfectionism

As Dr. Carroll notes, who we are and who we feel we should be may be unclear now, and ever-changing. Unless we solidly know who we are and what we stand for, we can easily fall prey to thinking we have to live up to someone else's definition of success. Personally, I am grateful that so many domains are now available to me as a woman. I would not have been happy being home every day, even though being a stay-at-home mom is an admirable occupation. I did try it for a few years after my first daughter was born, and I remember clearly, after a particularly frustrating day, my then husband looking at me lovingly and saying, "I think it's time for you to go back to work." He was right.

But it's not the number of domains we're trying to excel in that's the problem; perfectionism is the real enemy. If we are going to joyfully engage in many different domains in our lives, we must simply accept that there are domains where we will feel comfortable having lower standards.

Many years ago when I was completing my solution-focused coaching certificate at the University of Toronto, my instructor recalled a coaching session with a client. She asked the client where he felt he was right then in terms of a particular goal, on a scale of zero to 10, with 10 being achievement of the goal. His response: "6." Then she asked him where he would ideally like to be. His response: "6." He was content being at 6!

I thought, *Shouldn't we always be striving toward 10? Isn't that the only way to become excellent?* Then it dawned on me: if I wanted to reduce my stress and stay sane, I didn't have enough hours in the day to be a 10 in all the domains of my life. So I decided that I was going to choose in which domains I would strive for a 10 and in which domains I would strive for a 6 (or maybe lower). That's when I came up with the exercise I call "Peace at 6." It is one tool I use to reduce my need for perfectionism in so many domains of my life (I call myself a recovering perfectionist). For this and many of the exercises you'll find at the end of the chapters, you may want to use a notebook—for making notes and to practice each exercise.

EXERCISE: **PEACE AT 6**

Step 1: List the Important Domains in Your Life

On a piece of paper, draw a short line and then write down next to it a domain in your life that you feel is an important aspect of your life. Here is my list:

___ Exercise & Staying Fit
___ Eating Well
___ Recreation and Hobbies
___ Making Lots of Money
___ Family Relationships & Friendships
___ Romantic Relationships
___ Doing Good Work (my business)
___ Taking Care of the House (housework)
___ Volunteering in My Community
___ Making a Contribution to Society

Now create your list of all the life domains that are important to you. Only you can decide what is most important to you.

Step 2: Choose Three Life Domains That Are the Highest Priority for You

Which three domains will you choose to be highly invested in? Maybe your family relationships are extremely important to you and you want to dedicate most of your daily life to them—you want to strive to be a 10 in this area. That does not mean you will be disappointed if you are not a 10; this is just a sign that you will feel good about yourself and your life if you make it a priority. Assign a 10 to the three domains of your choosing. Be clear on what is *most* important to you.

Step 3: Assign a 6 to Every Other Domain

Now take a look at the other domains and assign to each a number that is 6 or lower. I know that is hard to do! This is about feeling comfortable with a lower standard. I took a look at all the domains in my life and decided that Family Relationships & Friendships, Making Lots of Money, and Doing Good Work would be the domains in which I will strive for a 10 right now. My priorities might change next year, but for now, this is where I want to focus my energy. Then I made a decision that I would be okay if I strived for a 6 in the other domains. That doesn't mean I don't find the other domains important; I am just choosing to be okay with a lower standard. Decide what a 6 (or lower) looks like to you. Go ahead. Try it and feel how liberating it is!

Step 4: Commit to Being Peaceful at 6

When I was assigning 6s, housework immediately came to mind. While I like to have a clean house, my house is constantly a mess. I guess having a perfect house just isn't a top priority for me and it never really has been. Now, don't get me wrong. If someone came in and waved a magic wand and made my house look perfectly designed and tidy, I would not object. It's just that, for me, keeping house is not my favorite activity.

So I immediately decided that no matter what was going on, I would be at peace if the state of my house was at a 6. That meant I had to give up my Lucy Ricardo–style of cleaning house. You may recall from the TV show *I Love Lucy* that Lucy would run around her apartment, cleaning everything just before guests came over. She'd stuff everything in the closet, and the place would soon look spotless. Inevitably, one of her guests would open the closet and everything would come crashing out on top of them.

That was my life too! Whenever my kids saw me tidying up, they would ask, "Mom, are people coming over?" To truly embrace being peaceful at 6, I had to surrender to the fact that sometimes people would come over and see my messy house.

At first it was difficult. I felt uncomfortable letting people see my mess. But I kept reminding myself that this was something I was doing to relieve my own stress. I stayed away from all things Martha Stewart. Letting the house be messy allowed me to flourish and feel better about myself. It gave me more positive mental energy for areas of my life where I wanted to be a 10. I stopped ruminating about the mess and learned to accept it.

I also decided that, while I wanted to be healthy, I didn't need to be exercising like a crazy person or eating healthily all the time. I love doing hot yoga every day, and some people ask me, "What about cardio?" Well, doing yoga every day works pretty darn well for me! I strive to eat healthy every day, but no one will deprive me of that piece of pizza or birthday cake. That meant I had to be okay with having a few extra pounds or having extra fat in certain places. I had to decide that not assigning 10s to the domains of Exercise & Staying Fit and Eating Well meant that my results in these domains would be less than 10, and I had to be okay with that.

So many of us don't put the time and effort into certain areas of our lives, and then we beat ourselves up over it. Decide that you will be peaceful about being at 6 no matter what the consequences. Do not beat yourself up for not being perfect. Letting go of perfectionism has been the most liberating thing I have done. When we are wanting things to be perfect, what we are really doing is striving for excellence, and that can be a positive thing in our lives. Just don't feel bad about yourself when things in your domains aren't perfect, because nothing ever is.

Step 4: Embrace Imperfection

Once you decide you will be peaceful at 6, embrace the domains in which you want to be a 10 and forget the rest. If you have made the choice to quit your career to be a stay-at-home mom while your kids are young, love it with all your being. Decide that for a while you will be a 6 in your career or in serving your community. Maybe you will need to set your number even lower than 6. Regretting the path you did not take will only zap your positive mental energy and prevent you from savoring how beautiful it is to be a stay-at-home mom. Decide to love yourself no matter what role you are in.

Eliminating perfectionism from your life allows you to consciously decide that you are "good enough" in certain areas where you feel comfortable operating at the standard that only you will set for yourself. It is deeply empowering to know that whatever the level you are at, you are enough. It's one way to stop doubting and start accepting yourself just as you are.

Confidence Habits

- Do not beat yourself up for having self-doubt. Our world is constantly changing, so having some self-doubt is normal. Decide that you will learn how to conquer it so it doesn't stop you from going after what you want—joyfully.
- Experiencing difficulties when embarking on new endeavors is common. Use your self-doubt to propel you to work harder and put more effort into reaching higher levels of performance. There is a difference between self-doubt and chronic self-doubt.
- Understand that you will never feel good enough if you are trying to be excellent in every domain of your life. Choose what you want to be excellent at and focus on that.
- Choose to let go of perfectionism.

3

How to Motivate Yourself to Conquer Self-Doubt (Yes, You Can Do It)

• • • • •

WHEN WE ARE highly motivated, no one has to convince, incent, or even pay us to do the task in question. We just do it. It's like with those people you know who have been physically fit their whole lives. You know there is no one at the end of their bed every morning yelling at them to exercise. They just get up and exercise every day.

Now imagine if you felt the same way about anything you are currently fearful of doing. Imagine if you felt no fear or hesitation—you just went out and did it. You know those people who started their own business, who chat up the cutest person at the bar, who keep writing amazing books, who run for office, who quit their job to travel the world? How did they go from being scared out of their minds to actually *doing* it? In this chapter we explore the science behind motivation.

What Is Motivation?

The *Merriam-Webster Learner's Dictionary* defines "motivation" as "a force or influence that causes someone to do something." There is a whole field of study in psychology known as self-determination theory (SDT), which focuses on the motivation behind the choices people make.[13] In psychological terms, motivation is the fuel that powers our behavior. Just as a car will not move if it has no gas, your mind will not move you to action if it is not motivated. Or, more plainly:

NO MOTIVATION = NO ACTION

It is important to understand that different things affect your motivation, including the way you think (the cognitive aspect), the way you feel (the emotional aspect), and subconscious motivators that are dictated by the way our brain works. Are you sometimes surprised why you're behaving in a particular way? Sometimes it's just because of the hardwiring of your brain.

Research in SDT focuses on two kinds of motivation: intrinsic and extrinsic. "Intrinsic motivation" refers to initiating an activity solely because it is enjoyable and satisfying. For example, I am intrinsically motivated to do hot yoga. Every day, I happily pencil it into my calendar because I enjoy it so much. No one has to persuade me to go. On the days I cannot attend class, I miss it.

"Extrinsic motivation" refers to engaging in an activity to get some external reward. For instance, I receive a commission for every person I sign up for a certain program I am involved with, and this money incents me to make more and better sales calls. I don't particularly enjoy making sales calls, but I do feel some satisfaction from enrolling more people in the program and making more money. This external reward drives my motivation to sell. I might be just as motivated to do something with an external motivator; it is just not enjoyable for its own sake. Also, if the external motivator is removed, I may not engage in the behavior.

Creating an external motivator can be helpful if you know yourself well enough to need one. When I married and had kids, I stopped making time for regular exercise. I wanted to get back on track, so I solicited the support of my friend Angela, who is an exerciser extraordinaire. Among other physical activity, Angela and I decided we would swim for an hour every Wednesday. I never missed my Wednesday swim times because I never wanted to disappoint Angela, and because she is a dedicated exerciser, she never missed a swim either. Angela was my extrinsic motivation.

If we truly want to understand how to push through our fears and do it joyfully, we need to learn how to increase our *intrinsic* motivation, because doing this will remove much of the psychological resistance we feel when we stop ourselves from going after what we want. If fear is the lock on the door that leads to the other side, then intrinsic motivation is the key that opens the door, removing the barrier, so we can freely go there. We cannot always rely on outside forces to motivate us. When we are intrinsically motivated, there is no resistance. We easily engage in the behaviors needed to be successful without any coaxing. We enjoy the process without anxiety and stress. We say *yes* to the things we really want to be doing with our lives.

According to Richard Ryan and Edward Deci, two leading SDT researchers, humans are driven by three psychological needs that contribute to intrinsic motivation, and that are essential for growth and well-being—just like sun, water, and soil are essential for plants to function optimally.[14]

1. Relatedness: The Universal Need to Interact, Be Connected to, and Experience Caring for Others

If we take into account all the well-being research, social connectedness is probably *the most* important contributing factor to well-being and happiness. We are social creatures. Having positive relationships in our lives is essential to our well-being.

Naomi Eisenberger, neuroscientist and professor in the social psychology program at the University of California, Los Angeles, and her colleagues conducted some very interesting studies that reveal we are hardwired for social connectedness.[15] Dr. Eisenberger explored what happened in research subjects' brains when they felt socially rejected. The subjects were wearing an fMRI cap so that the researchers could actually see what happened neurologically when rejection took place. The subjects were instructed to play a simple computer ball-tossing game with two avatars representing the research team. At one point in the game, the two avatars stopped playing with the research participant. At about the same time the person was excluded from the game, the regions of his or her brain that register and process physical pain were activated. The researchers referred to this as "social pain." Researchers hypothesize that thousands of years ago, human beings mainly survived in tribes. If you were kicked out of your tribe, you would probably die. We maintain these ancient parts of the brain, and researchers believe that being excluded triggers a response as if faced with a powerful threat to our survival.

Given this information, we can see how social connectedness can be a powerful motivator or demotivator for us. When we engage in certain activities or behaviors, we, to some degree, always want to know that we still "fit in" with our social circles. If our social group engages in particular behaviors, it's likely we will engage in them too. If our peers feel something's a good idea, it's much easier for us to jump in too. Equally, if this new behavior we want to engage in will be met with social disdain, we may not be so motivated to act on it.

At first, researchers believed that self-doubt was internally driven, but more and more they are discovering that self-doubt is inherently a social phenomenon. Self-doubt manifests from our concerns about social disapproval and the potential of being evaluated negatively by our peers, family, and others. Often people identify "fear of failure" as a strong demotivator, but if you dig a little deeper, it's failing in plain sight of your peers or other important people in your life that is the real fear. Thus, we may not engage in the behaviors that will allow us to fulfill our dreams for two reasons: fear of social evaluation, and fear of disapproval of others.

If we start to share our ideas and endeavors with those in our social circles, and they don't believe we can be successful (i.e., they think it's a "bad idea"), we may be filled with self-doubt. In fact, our brain is so sensitive to social disapproval that even a simple disapproving look from a loved one can trigger feelings that stop us from moving forward. This is why it may be best to refrain from sharing your great idea with your loved ones early on. Your confidence is most fragile at the beginning of any endeavor, so if people close to you shut you down early, your idea may never get off the ground.

Perhaps more surprisingly, for the same reasons, fear of success can also be a strong demotivator. I interviewed Tanya Geisler, a popular leadership coach in Toronto, and she highlighted that sometimes it is not fear of failure that holds us back but fear of shining brightly. For example, if you believe that becoming a rich and famous writer and speaker might intimidate your romantic partner, you might sabotage your own efforts for fear of losing them. If you think that being rich makes you a bad person in the eyes of your friends, you might not engage in activities that would make you financially successful. I often hear women say, "Oh, I don't do this for the money." There is nothing wrong with working and being paid for the value you bring. We are conditioned to think that if we ask for money in return for helping others (even when we are in helping professions), that somehow makes us look bad and damages our self-image. After talking to Tanya, I wondered about all the times I had dimmed my light so as not to alienate others.

Are you holding yourself back for fear of being judged by others in your life? Do you dim your light for fear those closest to you will leave you? Guess what. People may judge you, and they may not. People may leave you, and they may not. You must ask yourself, *Is it true?* Is it true your loved ones will leave you? Is it true your friends will stop speaking to you? Through open communication you can deal with the fears of your loved ones. Talk to them, ask them how they feel. You may be surprised.

Be prepared, though, for not getting the answers you are hoping for. This is a pivotal moment. How badly do you want this dream? How badly do you want to take your life in a new direction? If you don't go after this dream, how will you feel at the end of your life? Are your relationships holding you back? Only you can decide. We are hardwired for social connection, so do not underestimate how powerful a motivator that can be.

2. Autonomy: The Universal Urge to Be in Control of One's Own Life and Act in Harmony with What Is Important to Oneself

This human need is about having the freedom to engage in activities we feel are aligned with our life's purpose and our values. If we feel passionate about a certain cause, we are highly motivated and would do almost anything to pursue it. Think of Malala Yousafzai, the renowned teenaged activist who won a Nobel Peace Prize for her fearless and tireless work to gain access to education for the more than 30 million girls who are denied an education. Despite her being shot in the head by a Taliban gunman at the age of fifteen—and surviving—she continues to pursue her dream of education for everyone on the planet. I don't know about you, but if I were shot in the head for the work I do, I would be packing my bags and leaving town! Not Malala. Being shot was like rocket fuel for her cause. Passion can be a powerful motivator indeed.

Sometimes we pursue goals for the wrong reasons. I grew up believing that money was the most important measure of one's success. I thought I needed lots of money and a fancy house in order for my family to value me. So I pursued a degree in business because I felt that was the best way to make money. My first job out of university was selling computers at IBM, as I knew I could make a lot of money in sales. And I did. But I hated the job. I enjoyed the people I worked with, and I learned a lot from working at IBM, but I was not passionate about selling computers. After six years, I decided to leave the job. My friends and colleagues asked me why I was quitting. I told them I didn't enjoy it. They were surprised. "But you're so good at selling," they said. They had mistaken my skills for my passion.

While I was at IBM, the company offered a career-counseling course to help employees discover their most desired career goals. Ironically, instead of focusing my goals on a career at IBM, the course helped me discover that career counseling was a personal passion—I wanted to help others discover their passions. So I left IBM and started to build my career-coaching practice. The sales skills came in handy, because when you go out on your own, you need to know how to sell your services if you are going to make a living. I also found the skill useful to teach other independent consultants how to sell their services—while many consultants loved the consulting part, they were not so good at the selling part. I had taken something I was good at and changed the focus toward an audience I was passionate about helping. It was a perfect fit for me.

If you want to be truly motivated, you have to connect with the *reasons why* you are pursuing your goals. Are you going after them for someone else because that person believes these goals are the best thing for you? Or because your family would disapprove if you didn't? Or because accomplishing these goals will make you look good in front of your peers? If you answered yes to any of these questions, perhaps your goals are not truly aligned with your inner values. If you are always focused on goals that are based on others' agendas, you cannot tap into that truly powerful motivation for what is authentically important to you.

Well-being researchers have discovered that *self-concordant goals*—goals that are aligned with our true and authentic self and have personal meaning for us—are motivating. We are more likely to expend consistent effort toward them over time than we are toward goals that are not aligned with our true self. Higher levels of well-being and happiness are also associated with setting and pursuing self-concordant goals. When we are autonomously driven by our passions and by goals that are self-concordant, the achievement of these goals becomes motivating and satisfying.

3. Competence: A Need to Control the Outcome of Our Actions and Experience Mastery

We all have a deep human need to feel we have acquired enough skill and knowledge to be accomplished and capable. When we feel we are competent in a certain skill or activity, we feel motivated to engage in it again and again. I started public speaking in Grade 6, and won the first speech contest I participated in. I always enjoyed giving presentations at work or participating in company skits when I worked at IBM. But when, in my thirties, I began my own consulting practice, I didn't think I was good enough to actually be paid to be a professional speaker. When people suggested I come and speak at their companies, I wouldn't follow up. I shied away from opportunities because I felt so anxious about public-speaking engagements.

I started doing some small corporate workshops and soon became more comfortable as a professional speaker. As a result, I got better and better at it and my competence started to rise. Once I gained enough mastery in my public-speaking abilities, I felt less anxious and more energized with every talk I delivered. When people contacted me, I sent them proposals right away, to secure the business. That is because *intrinsic motivation increases with the feeling of competency*. If someone asked you to do something that you know you are good at—even excel at—you'd jump in without hesitation. For example, if someone asked me to bring a lasagna to a potluck dinner, I would happily oblige because I know I make a good lasagna (my Sicilian mother taught me well). I think of past times I've brought lasagna and it got a lot of compliments. But if I were asked me to make a curry, I would say no, because I have never made one before and I wouldn't want people to be disappointed with the dish I brought. Even though I would like to learn how to make a good curry and this would be a perfect opportunity to try, I picture everyone at the potluck leaving it uneaten on their plate and so would shy away from making it. When we have confidence in our competence in a certain area, we engage easily without fear of potential embarrassment.

Positive feedback about a job well done increases our feelings of competence and motivates us to do more. We have a basic human need and desire for growth and development, and positive accomplishment is an important pillar of happiness. We want to achieve and master challenges, and inherently those achievements become part of who we are.

So if feeling competent motivates us, and not feeling competent demotivates us, you can see why you may shy away from pursuing something brand new to you. Thus, a lack of competence in a new skill or endeavor can work against us. And that is why you cannot wait to feel confident in order to engage in something new—because in the beginning it can be hard, and it can be messy. Basic psychology tells us that we will most likely feel uncomfortable at this beginning stage and that our confidence will be low. The trick is to be aware, recognize that it is deeply human to feel this way, and move forward anyway!

Nothing kills feelings of competence faster than self-doubt. We have such a powerful desire to appear competent all the time that we engage in self-protective behaviors when something threatens how competent we appear. These behaviors can sabotage us when we are trying to pursue important goals. A great deal of research examines the relationship between chronic self-doubt and certain self-protective behaviors—coping strategies. If you want to truly move beyond self-doubt, you need to come to a deeper understanding of how it may be showing up in your daily life.

Six Common Coping Strategies Caused by Self-Doubt

When we are experiencing self-doubt about our competence, we tend to get defensive and protect ourselves from undesired outcomes in order to preserve our feelings of self-worth. When I discovered these coping strategies in the research literature, I realized that I myself had engaged in each and every one.[16] I review these problematic behaviors here in the hope that your knowing about them will allow you to manage them. In later chapters, I discuss effective strategies for overcoming them. See if you can recognize yourself in any of these behaviors, and remember: these are highly human and common to us all.

1. Self-Handicapping

Self-handicapping occurs when we deliberately undermine our performance in some task or endeavor, thereby increasing the likelihood of failure, in an attempt to obscure the reason for failure. For example, if I am feeling very unsure about my ability to deliver an amazing keynote, I may go out the night before and get very drunk. The next morning, when I am completely hungover and my speech is just a so-so performance, I can tell myself and others around me that my low level of performance was not a result of my own ineptitude but because I was hungover as hell. Hence my self-image is protected, and I am still feeling good about myself.

This strategy does not overcome self-doubt but merely helps you cope with it, as it sabotages success. Our desire to protect our self-image is so strong, we would rather plan to fail than face the potential embarrassment of unexpectedly failing in front of others. An artist at one of my workshops told me that every time she is about to get involved with a big art show, she becomes ill and has to withdraw. This had happened four times in a row—it was a pattern. It is amazing how our self-doubt can not only control our behaviors but also affect our physiology!

In one interesting study, researchers had participants in one group work on some very difficult and unsolvable problems.[17] After the test, researchers gave the participants enthusiastic feedback and high praise. Now the participants were perplexed: on the one hand, they clearly felt they had not done well on the test; on the other hand, they were labeled as successful anyway. The participants were then told that they were going to retest but, this time, they could first take a drug that would enhance their performance or a drug that would hinder their performance. Can you guess which the likeliest choice was? A higher percentage of men (but, interestingly, not of the women) chose the hindering drug. The men were not certain how to reproduce a successful outcome, so accepting the self-handicap gave them an opportunity to protect the image they had already established—that of a highly intelligent human being—rather than risk failure. This is a classic example of self-handicapping in action.

2. Impostor Phenomenon

Impostor phenomenon, also known as "impostor syndrome," is a term coined by clinical psychologists Pauline Clance and

Anything I've ever done that ultimately was worthwhile initially scared me to death.

BETTY BENDER

Suzanne Imes.[18] This phenomenon occurs when a high-achieving individual is incapable of attributing their achievements to their own talent or skills and has ongoing feelings of being a fraud. Any success they have is dismissed as good luck or due to their ability to deceive others into believing that they are more intelligent and talented than they really are. Unlike the self-handicapper, who obscures the reason for failure, people experiencing the impostor phenomenon obscure the reason for their success. Consequently, they never have an opportunity to reinforce their beliefs that they are increasingly becoming more competent, thereby negatively affecting their motivation and future performance.

Impostor phenomenon is particularly troubling, as it constantly perpetuates self-doubt. The only way to move from self-doubt into feelings of greater confidence is to shift your beliefs toward mastery. That is, until you believe you are getting better at something, you will never increase your confidence levels. Researchers call this "attribution." If you are constantly attributing your success to some outside source and never to your intelligence or talent, you will never shift your core beliefs or feel confident in your abilities. It's not enough to do the work and improve. You must *believe* that you are improving and your successful performance is because of your efforts.

3. Procrastination

One important contributor for motivating us toward our goals is our *outcome expectancies*. If we expect the outcome of our actions to be success we more easily engage in the behaviors and tasks necessary to achieve our goals. If we expect the outcome of our actions to be failure, we may not be motivated to put in the effort required to be successful. This scenario is particularly the case when our performance will be socially evaluated—for example, writing a book, displaying personal art, or acting in a play.

We attempt to protect our self-worth by procrastinating. Procrastination allows us to delay a task when we know our performance will be socially evaluated. As human beings we are often more focused and concerned with how our performance will be judged than with the success of the performance itself.

Here's an example to explain how self-doubt and procrastination are related. I had been talking about writing a book for ten years. Talking about the book was safe and pleasant. People were excited to hear about it, and my proposed topics (which have changed over the years) were interesting. But I never actually prioritized writing the book. I wasn't making the time because once I actually wrote and published the book, I would leave myself open to social evaluation at a greater scale. In other words, now people from *all around the world* could tell me the book is amazing, the book is so-so, or the book is terrible. Many authors share this fear: once they put their ideas out there, they worry, *What will people think?* or *How will I look?* Prolonging social evaluation for as long as I could—procrastinating—was a great strategy for staying in the safe zone. It also explains my nonperformance for so many years.

4. "Other" Enhancement

When we engage in a performance that easily compares us to others, we may highlight some advantage our opponents or competitors have that we ourselves did not have the privilege to enjoy. For example, the CPPA runs a conference every year with almost no funding from any universities or corporate sponsors. As a result, we cannot invite many of the biggest names in positive psychology because we simply can't afford to pay their fees. So when I compare our conference to other conferences that have ten or so big names, I comfort myself in thinking that they obviously have some greater funding source than we do. "Other" enhancement is not necessarily a bad strategy, as it allows people to perform their best and still feel okay about their overall performance, even if they do not do as well as others.

Enhancing others is a problem when we use it as an excuse for nonaction—when it fuels our belief that, since we do not have the advantages others have, we will never achieve the same levels. So why try at all, then? I have heard people say things like "Well, Louisa, I don't have a master's degree like you" or "I'm not young like them; I can't possibly start now." These excuses are powerful because they "justify" people's decisions to not pursue their goals. By always believing that other speakers probably had more credentials than I had, I stopped myself from going after my dream of becoming a professional speaker.

Many years ago, before I began my speaking career, I met with Grace Cirocco, a popular speaker in Toronto. I did not feel I had any credentials, and I wanted to learn more about the credentials required to be a professional speaker. She was very helpful, describing all of her education and experience that got her to where she was, but she could see I was still feeling discouraged. She looked me straight in the eye and said, "Do you think Tony Robbins has any fancy university degrees? You don't need a degree to speak. Just give yourself the permission!" It was a profound moment for me that shifted my thinking. When I went home that day, I looked it up. Tony Robbins does not have any fancy degrees. I also discovered that Bill Gates didn't either when he started Microsoft. Ellen DeGeneres did not go to college, and apparently Rachel Ray did not go to culinary school. These people merely had natural talents, believed in themselves, and weren't afraid to put themselves out there. Don't let the enhancement of others stop you from going after what you really want. There is always a route to get you there.

5. Subjective Overachievement

Sometimes people expend heroic amounts of effort to absolutely guarantee success. Of all the strategies I have used to overcome my own self-doubt, subjective overachievement is probably the one I've used most often. In my huge desire to be successful and meet my goals, I overwork and overprepare. When organizing our first Canadian Conference on Positive Psychology, in 2012, I drove myself and my team to exhaustion to get everything right and execute our vision so that it was of the highest possible quality. Now we would all admit it was a hugely successful conference and it was executed without a hitch, but I was worn-out, stressed, and feeling like I would never organize another conference again.

Subjective overachievement almost always guarantees success, but it is exhausting and actually lowers your well-being over time. Also, once you attribute your successful outcomes to the overexpenditure of effort and resources, you continue to use this strategy because it works for you—thereby continuing to exhaust yourself. By overcoming self-doubt and believing that your success is not only attributed to your hard work *but also to your talents and abilities*, you can begin to expend the *appropriate* amount of effort, making life feel more manageable and balanced.

6. Defensive Pessimism

Defensive pessimism is a strategy people use to protect themselves against a possible future failure, thereby managing anxiety and fear. This strategy is not one by which you turn into a general pessimist, but rather you approach a stressful task with a certain amount of pessimism. Defensive pessimists set low expectations for themselves and thus are better able to anticipate everything that can go wrong. Then they put a plan in place to prepare for the worst, giving themselves a sense of peace and control over the situation and reducing their anxiety. By anticipating you might fail for good reason, you are also not so devastated should failure be the outcome. An expected failure is much easier for us to accept than an unexpected failure.

Dr. Julie Norem, psychology professor at Wellesley College, in Massachusetts, has studied and written extensively about defensive pessimism.[19] If, instead of being immobilized by the anxiety caused by self-doubt, you put a plan in place to deal with each possible setback as you engage in an important task, this can actually help you perform better. You feel more confident that you can deal with whatever comes your way. For example, when I first started to deliver my own workshops, I had a great deal of self-doubt and worried that the workshop would bomb. So for every topic I introduced in the workshop, I'd read an entire book on the topic or engage in hours of research on the Internet—just in case anyone asked me a question about it. I spent a great deal of time preparing, reading, and reviewing everything "just in case." It helped me reduce my anxiety.

Defensive pessimism may help deal with anxiety over the short term, which helps us perform better, but this strategy has some drawbacks. If we are always in a chronic state of anxiety as we approach new goals, research in neurobiology suggests, this will eventually deteriorate our physical health. Unless we can successfully address the root cause of our anxiety, this vicious cycle will continue, detracting from our well-being and happiness. The best way to joyfully move forward toward our dreams is by reducing and managing the doubt.

Time for Change

Have you engaged in any of the behaviors discussed above? Can you see how self-doubt may be interfering with your ability to pursue your goals and dreams? I still sometimes find myself falling into these traps, but now I can quickly catch myself and reset my course of action. At the heart of every one of these behaviors is the notion that we are constantly protecting our self-image from hurt or harm. We have to stop believing that everything we do is a reflection of who we are as individuals and realize that it's more a reflection of the amount of effort we put into accomplishing. Once we do that, we might not be so focused on protecting our self-image all the time.

If you engage in these behaviors regularly, it is important to recognize what triggers them and make a change. Dr. Carroll explains that once we discover that a certain self-doubt coping strategy works for us, we may use it over and over again, even subconsciously. Being a subjective overachiever worked for me. Once I started to become more authentically confident about my abilities in delivering workshops and trusted that the reason for my success was not my hours of preparation but my competence, I stopped putting such enormous effort into the prep. Soon after, I started to enjoy my prep time without anxiety. I had greater balance in my life, as I was putting the *appropriate* amount of time and effort into the workshop prep. I also had greater peace of mind as I went about my work. Let me share with you a story about a simple but effective technique for zapping anxiety about an upcoming task and getting moving forward fast.

"So What?"

When I graduated from university I applied for a job at IBM as a sales representative. There were some twelve hundred other candidates and only five positions available, so I did things to stand out from the crowd. My boyfriend at the time worked for IBM, and he would sneak into the office in the middle of the night and leave letters on the decision maker's keyboard for me (this was pre-email days). I would also call the HR Department periodically to remind them of my interest in the job. I wanted to work for IBM so badly, and I was thrilled when, three months later, I landed one of those five positions.

On my first day, my manager gave me three large boxes filled with technical books and articles and instructed me to read them all, saying, "In three weeks, you'll have to write an exam on all this. If you get lower than 70 percent on the exam, we'll reconsider whether we still want to employ you." Needless to say, I was stressed. I had to learn and memorize hundreds and hundreds of pages about everything from bits and bytes to each model of computer IBM sold and all the features. Much of this techy stuff was new to me. As exam day approached I panicked even more. *What if I don't pass? What if they fire me?* I continued to study day and night, but on the morning of the exam, I was so distraught I was crying. I wasn't sure I could pull it off. I was still living at home, and as I left that morning, my mother stopped me.

"Are you crying?" she asked.

"Yes," I responded through my sobs.

"What are you crying about?"

"I'm so worried about this exam. If I don't get at least 70 percent on it, IBM might fire me!"

Then my mother said something I will never forget.

"So what?!"

"So what? What do you mean, so what? I could lose my job!" I couldn't believe she had said that.

But she said it again. "So what? Lots of companies wanted to hire you after you graduated. If IBM doesn't want you, I'm sure there are lots of companies that do!"

My panic suddenly disappeared. She was right. Was it really the end of the world if I didn't pass the exam? I was still living at home and had good prospects. If I did lose my job, I could reach out to the other companies that wanted to hire me. Those two words allowed me to relax and just do my best. I passed the exam and went on to become a sales rep. Since then I have used my mom's "So what?" technique many times when feeling anxious.

Passing the "So What?" Test

How often do you stop yourself from doing something because you are anxious and fearful about the outcome? Perhaps you've just received a job offer and you're afraid to negotiate for a higher salary because you are afraid of what your new employer might say. In fact, one study found that only 7 percent of female graduating students attempted to negotiate their initial compensation offer, compared with 57 percent of men.[20] Those who negotiated gained on average 7.4 percent over their initial offers. The next time you are stressed about a certain outcome, ask yourself, *So what if I fail? So what if they say no? What's the worst that could happen?* Usually the worst is really not that bad. If you ask for a higher starting salary and are told no, you are no worse off than before you asked.

If you think there is a likelihood the worst could happen, prepare for it. If you are worried that asking for a higher starting salary might sour relations with your new employer, plan the best way to negotiate. Think of the salary that you believe is appropriate, and think of three things that might justify this higher salary from the start. If you're told no, perhaps you can set yourself up for a review in three months' time, after you've had a chance to prove your worth. Consult with a trusted adviser or mentor who can help you navigate. I had to negotiate a new kind of project once and I didn't know what to charge my client, so I called a good friend who charges a much higher fee than I do. He helped me see my worth, and we brainstormed on the right number. We also discussed the rationale behind the number. I went back to the client with that number, which was double what I had originally planned to present, and the client didn't even blink. Huge success! So don't be afraid to go all the way with this one.

The "So what?" technique might also lead you in the opposite direction. If you suspect you cannot recover from the worst scenario, maybe another route would be better for you. Of course, I am not talking about life-or-death situations. I sometimes believe that if the worst does happen, it was meant to be. Someone asked me if I was afraid of criticism about my book. So I asked myself, *So what if my book receives criticism?* Here is how I responded to my own question:

- "Even the best books out there get criticized by someone. Not everyone is going to like this book, and that's okay."

- "Do you think Oprah thinks about calling it quits just because someone criticizes her? She has lots of criticizers and still has a thriving empire!"
- "If I am criticized, I will deal with the criticism as it comes. I might even learn more about this topic from the information my criticizers share."
- "My book doesn't need to be perfect. I'm just adding to the conversation."

When you say "So what?" to your fear, it loses steam. It's almost like popping a balloon. Whereas criticism seemed like this scary thing before, now it's no big deal. Sometimes you fear you just won't be able to handle it if the worst were to happen, but you are stronger and more resilient than you think. Even if your endeavor leads to failure, you need to be proud that you had the courage to face your fears. Doing what is right is not always comfortable, but nothing worth fighting for is all of the time. You are a strong woman, and you deserve to go after your dreams.

You may be perplexed about why you are holding yourself back. This might be because you don't know what the real fear is. So the first step is to become aware. The other day I found myself avoiding a contract I had to finalize for an important project I was working on. I was anxious about it and kept putting it off. Then I came to the realization that I could be potentially self-sabotaging the whole thing. I simply asked the question, "Am I self-sabotaging?" When I realized this might be the case, I peeled one more layer and began to explore what it was about that particular project that was making me fearful. Once I named my fear, I created a plan that made me feel much better about the whole thing and then started to do what needed to be done to get that contract signed.

Here is an exercise that will allow you to explore your behaviors and the fears that feed into them.

EXERCISE: **TAME THAT FEAR**

1. Take a moment to reflect on the past month or two, and ask yourself if you have engaged in any of the six self-protective, coping strategies as described above:
   a. Self-handicapping
   b. Impostor phenomenon
   c. Procrastination
   d. "Other" enhancement
   e. Subjective overachievement
   f. Defensive pessimism
2. In a journal, identify the coping strategy and describe the times this has happened and what it was in regard to. What tasks were you engaged in? What goals were you trying to achieve? What behaviors did you engage in? Try to describe in detail how you were derailing yourself or how these behaviors were getting in the way of your success.

3. Ask yourself, *What is the real fear here?* Really dig and write down what you come up with. For example, if you are procrastinating on starting your own coaching business, what is the fear around that? If you are a subjective overachiever, what are you anxious and fearful about when you put all that energy into your work? It is important to get crystal clear on what the underlying fear is.

4. Once you have named the real fear, create a plan that will tame that fear. For example, if you are fearful about starting a coaching business because you're unsure whether you can bring in enough clients, you might start by taking a marketing course for coaches. Perhaps you could subcontract for other coaches who have too much business. This will give you a chance to learn more about the business before striking out on your own. If you are putting enormous effort into a certain project because you feel you just don't have the experience required to do a good job, could you take a course to get deeper knowledge on the topic? Perhaps you need to pursue a certificate, to take your skills to a higher level.

5. What is important is to identify one small step you can take toward taming the fear, rather than one small step you can take toward the goal. By reducing the fears around goals, you erase the resistance—you will see that you begin to naturally move toward them. You are trying to erase barriers here by addressing the fear before going after the goal.

6 Over the next two weeks, be keenly aware of when any of these six problematic behaviors pop up for you. Make note of what triggers them, and use the same technique to tame your fears.

Confidence Habits

- Set goals that align with your authentic self. Do not focus your life on other people's agendas.
- Spend more time building your competence rather than protecting your self-worth, as this will build intrinsic motivation, which in turn will reduce the resistance you have to moving toward goals.
- Learn to become aware of when you are engaging in any of the six problematic behaviors—the self-protective coping strategies caused by self-doubt—and set a new course. Becoming aware is the first step toward change.
- Tame your fears, as this will remove the resistance that is stopping you from moving toward your goals.
- Say *So what?* to your fears more often, and just go for it!

4

How to Say Yes When Your Brain Is Saying No

IN THE PREVIOUS chapter, we discussed how building competence can increase our motivation to move into action more easily. In order to build competence, you actually have to practice what you want to improve. But many people stop themselves from even trying new things because they don't have enough confidence. Do you know how many times people have said to me, "Oh Louisa, I don't have the confidence to do that!"?

Marie Forleo, an influential businesswoman and Web TV host, once said, "Confidence is overrated. If you wait until you feel confident to start anything, you're never going to start anything."[21] This is especially true when embarking on a new venture. How can you feel confident if you have never done it before? So it's not confidence you need to get started; it's courage.

I had the pleasure of interviewing Robert Biswas-Diener, positive psychologist and happiness researcher, about his book

The Courage Quotient.[22] He claims that in order to move into action, your willingness to act must be greater than your fear. We just need to be able to muster up enough courage to take that first step. If any of you have seen a baby take its first steps, you will know it is not pretty or graceful. Luckily, babies are not thinking, *Oh geez, I wonder if I'm going to look like an idiot taking my first step*. Instead they are probably thinking, *I see everyone else walking on two legs, that looks pretty cool. I think I will give it a try*. They stumble and fall and get back up and flail around. They use the sofa to support them. It does not occur to them to be self-conscious about how they look while learning to walk. They usually have a couple of proud parents or siblings nearby cheering them, maybe even videotaping them. After many more months of practicing, they eventually learn how to walk quite confidently.

The problem with adults is that we are not willing to show others our awkward "baby step" phase. It's too embarrassing. Or we go out, take a baby step, it goes horribly wrong, and our brain protects us by searing that into our memory so we don't try it again. Or we think it will ruin our careers or destroy our credibility. We want to go out perfectly the first time. And it is this need we have to be good at something even on the first try that blocks us from starting.

Some psychologists believe that you should not focus on confidence but, rather, on building competence, because this is what boosts self-confidence. This is true, but developing competence takes time, and you need the positive mental energy to sustain you while you work on becoming reasonably competent at something. What about all that negative mind chatter saying, *You can't do that!* or *What if I look like an idiot trying?* or *I have no idea how I can get good at something like this.* These voices may stop you, make you hesitate, or perhaps even convince you to give up on your goals. It is that deciding moment that I want to focus on. I want to help you choose *Yes, I'm going to try it* instead of *No, I'm too scared.* That pivotal moment is what I refer to as the *courage to act.*

The Moment to Act Is Now, Because Regret Is More Powerful Than You Think

Often we put off pursuing our most desired and biggest goals because fear of failure in the moment seems to outweigh the current benefits of pursuing it. Failure is a very strong demotivator for us, so if we have an opportunity to avoid it in the present moment, we do. That's just how our brain is wired. When we have a bad experience, one that brings negative emotions, our brain codes it as bad and in future we try to avoid a recurrence. Equally, when we have a good experience, one that brings positive emotions, our brain codes it as good and we are more likely to easily engage in that activity again. When we even just think about taking a certain risk and possible failure, our imagination may run away with us, until catastrophizing gets the better of us. Catastrophic thinking is irrationally imagining a much worse possible outcome than is probably realistic. As discussed in chapter 3, we are highly sensitive to social approval, so the thought of failing in front of others might bring such an emotional response that it is hard to think rationally about what it is we want to embark on. We may know intellectually that there is no threat, but our emotions are fueling our behavior and we are saying no to the very thing we wish we could say yes to. So now our brain is working against us as we try to move toward our most desired (yet scariest) goals. In the moment it seems most comfortable to refrain from moving forward. No risk taken, self-worth protected. We are safe.

Now fast-forward to your deathbed. You are reflecting on that one dream you had that you never went after. What do you think is worse? The regret you feel by taking a risk and having it fail, or the regret you feel at the end of your life that you never even tried? Regret over things we did *not* do are worse at end of life.

Research shows that human beings are actually very bad predictors of how much and for how long failure will affect us, and we tend to overestimate its effects. We also underestimate how much we'll regret not having done something. Research by Victoria Medvec, a professor of management and organization at the Kellogg School of Management, shows that with the passage of time, we become more focused on opportunities not taken than on opportunities taken, even if they resulted in failure.[23] For example, someone at the end of life may regret never asking that special person out on a date and always wonder *What if?*

Knowing this, how can you overcome the urge to run screaming from possible failure? The only way is to accept that when you try something new, you will feel uncomfortable until you reach some level of mastery. The key to beginning is to sit in the discomfort and do it anyway. And when you begin, despite your fears, guess what? You improve your competence, which fuels your confidence. In the meantime, you need to call upon your mental resources to get you through that fearful gap. Let me offer you a bridge.

Engage in Small Yeses

You do not necessarily have to start with one big decision. Remember, success comes not with one big yes but with hundreds of smaller yeses along the way. Let's say you want to lose weight. This goal requires you to regulate what you eat every day, and make a choice every time you think about eating. Do I have my coffee black, or with cream and sugar? Do I have fried eggs with bacon and buttered toast, or choose poached eggs and fruit instead? Do I order salad with lean chicken, or my favorite grilled-cheese sandwich with fries? It is not an earth-shattering event that maintains your weight or causes weight loss or gain. It is one small decision at a time, one small shift in your thinking. If every time you have to make that decision you say to yourself, *This morning I will have my coffee with cream and sugar, but tomorrow I'll have it black* or *For lunch this time I will have the fries, but I'll eat less for dinner*, you are putting off your decision to eat well and you will not achieve your desired weight-loss goal.

Instead, every time you are sitting with that damn uncomfortable decision, realize that this is the moment. This tiny decision will make or break your diet. You have a chance to make that decision several times a day. Losing the weight requires that consciousness and strength. Over time, those positive decisions add up and voilà, some months later, you have lost the weight.

The same applies to increasing your courage. When faced with that decision to rise to the occasion and take a risk (which might lead to failure or disappointment or social embarrassment), you have to understand that this is your moment. It might be easy to say, "There will be another opportunity tomorrow. It's too scary right now" or "I'm not in the best place to make this decision, I'm too busy... I'll do it next week." That is the moment you have to picture yourself in the future regretting decisions you did not make in the present. Choose the short-term pain or challenge—which, by the way, might actually be less scary than you think. You might find that what appeared to be impossible was completely achievable. You might even... wait for it... succeed on your first try! Or maybe the first try is a disappointment but you learn so much from it that it will help you achieve success the next time, and the next time. Remember that it might take several tries.

Start by asking yourself, "What is a small yes?" Recognize when one small opportunity to say yes is staring you in the face, and start to chip away at your fear. If you're too scared to ask someone out on a date, a small yes might be to engage in friendly chitchat with strangers in the food court. If public speaking is too scary for you, you might start by asking if you can be the person to thank the speaker at the end of their talk. If you're too afraid to start your own business, maybe you do a bit of work for a friend who is running their own business.

Identify what those small yeses are for you, and start finding opportunities to act on them.

That moment when you have the chance to say yes is powerful. Own it. Be sure to have an excellent friend ready to pick you up if you fall, someone you can call and tell, "I was pushing the envelope and took a risk, and I blew it. But I am so proud that I took the risk that I wanted to share my win with you." Make sure it's a friend who knows what you are trying to achieve.

Magical Thinking

I asked Robert Biswas-Diener for his favorite courage-building technique. His response: "Magical thinking."

Magical thinking is the belief that something or someone will bring you luck or good fortune. Similar to superstitions like saying "Break a leg" before a big performance or carrying a rabbit's foot for good luck. What is fascinating is that in research experiments where people had to perform certain tasks, those who had engaged in good-luck superstitions such as knocking on wood or carrying a lucky charm actually performed better than those who didn't activate superstitions.[24] What the researchers found is that performance benefits were produced by boosts in participants' confidence and self-efficacy in mastering these tasks, which in turn improved performance. Since self-efficacy is more about our *beliefs* rather than our capabilities, this makes sense. (I discuss self-efficacy in more detail later in this chapter.) Many people believe that different crystals bring certain energies or certain displays of numbers (11:11, say) offer special powers. Symbols, statues, prayer beads, game shorts, your shirt turned inside out—the list goes on and on. I am sure you have your own forms of "magical thinking" that you believe bring you strength when you need it.

My mother used to go to church every day. For her, prayer was a powerful source of strength and resilience. My mother passed away in August 2015 and a clairvoyant friend told me that my mom would send feathers as a sign that she was still with me. I cannot tell you how many times tiny feathers have fallen randomly from the bathroom ceiling or cascaded in the air in front of me, to land gently on my keyboard as I wrote this book.

While I was on a writer's retreat at a cottage in Muskoka, north of Toronto, I took a break to go swim in the lake. I was in the water when suddenly I felt my mother's spiritual presence. I quickly looked to my right to see if there was a feather sign from her. Nothing. So I turned to my left and saw that no more than a foot behind me was a duck. Yes, a duck full of feathers! I began to swim, and this duck swam right next to me for ten minutes. This is very unusual behavior for a duck—ducks are typically scared of humans and keep their distance. I cannot explain what happened that day, but for me it was magical, and these magical powers are a source of strength and inspiration. I just knew in that moment that my mother was with me, encouraging me, supporting me, uplifting me while I wrote this book. That is powerful and is as yet another source of strength for me.

Now, I know this may sound kind of woo-woo to those of you with a scientific understanding of confidence and human behavior. But after all the thousands of pages of scientific research I have read, there is one thing I know for sure and that is that *we don't know what we don't know*. So if something gives you strength and you can't explain it, be open to receiving its confidence-building power. It may just work for you.

Now let's explore the terms scientists use when talking about confidence. Understanding these terms and the differences between them is important if you really want to understand human motivation and what gives us the courage to act in any given moment.

Self-Esteem

For decades, psychologists thought that, to be successful, we needed high self-esteem. Most researchers define self-esteem as a global evaluation of the self and one's self-worth; it is a judgment about yourself at any given time—Do I feel I am a good person, or do I feel I am a bad person? Do I feel good about myself, or do I feel bad about myself?

Psychologists will not argue that having a healthy level of self-esteem is a good thing. Research shows that low levels of self-esteem are correlated with depression and anxiety. Thus, self-esteem is important for our overall psychological well-being. But there is very little research to support the idea that high self-esteem drives performance. In fact, pursuing high self-esteem can actually be detrimental to your performance.

When I started to have children, the self-esteem movement had just begun. Educators everywhere believed that building a child's self-esteem was the most important contributing factor to success. So they started to be careful about hurting a child's feelings by failing them in school or criticizing them. Children's sports associations started having "festivals" instead of competitions, not keeping score and giving trophies to everyone, so that kids on the losing teams didn't get their feelings hurt. Researchers are now discovering that the movement has done more harm than good. I could write a whole other book on this topic alone, but here I want to talk about how focusing on building self-esteem can harm your chances of success.

Dr. Jennifer Crocker at Ohio State University proposes that "the importance of self-esteem lies more in how people strive for it rather than whether it is high or low."[25] When people focus too much of their energy on feeling good about themselves, they spend an inordinate amount of time engaging in activities that validate their abilities and qualities; in other words, their self-esteem. Dr. Crocker refers to this as "contingent self-esteem." If I feel good about myself because I see myself as an intelligent student, my self-esteem goes up when I get an A at school, and it goes down when I get a C. It does not necessarily go up or down if I win or lose a tennis match, because my self-esteem is not invested in my tennis skills.

So, if my self-worth is highly invested in the idea that I am an intelligent student, my self-esteem is now contingent on my grades. So in future I may pursue only courses where I know I will excel, even though taking a course in a different subject might actually be better for my career. Also, if I am halfway through the course and getting a C, I may drop the course before it affects my record—it's easier for me to tell people I

People with high assurance in their capabilities approach difficult tasks as challenges to be mastered rather than as threats to be avoided.

DR. ALBERT BANDURA

quit rather than risk failing. The short-term emotional benefits that come from boosts in self-esteem can be so appealing that we don't engage in other, more challenging pursuits that will get us closer to reaching our goals.

The pursuit of self-esteem can interfere with your learning and skill mastery, which is the only way you are going to excel at anything. If you are always trying to validate your self-worth, you are going to avoid potential failures, criticism, and negative feedback, rather than seeing them as opportunities to learn and grow. The best way to build self-confidence is to go out and master what it is you want to accomplish. Get better and better at it. Mistakes, failures, criticism, and feedback of any kind are exactly what you need to take yourself to the next level. You have to be able to look at an accomplishment and decide that it is a learning opportunity, not something that is just going to give your image a shiny boost.

Another pitfall of contingent self-esteem is feeling bad about ourselves after a setback or failure, which does not help us stay motivated to try again. In fact, it will zap your positive mental energy, the energy you need to persevere. In order for us not to make our self-esteem contingent on our successful achievements, we have to decide that our self-worth or self-esteem will not be affected by our failures or setbacks. In other words, do not take the failure personally. Feel good about yourself no matter what, and focus on how you will get better at the task. If you want to be on top of your game, you have to focus on growing and learning and forget the rest. Self-esteem alone is not going to get you there.

Self-Confidence

Self-confidence is the belief that you can do things well or succeed. It is a general feeling that you have the capacity to cope in most situations. Self-esteem and self-confidence are related, but you could have one without the other. You might not be feeling confident about engaging in a certain activity but still feel good about yourself. Many researchers would argue that confidence is a motivator, but for the sake of this discussion, I want to get even more detailed here.

I have healthy self-esteem. I feel good about myself as a person, and I feel quite confident about myself and my abilities. I feel that I can cope with whatever comes my way. But when it comes to dating in this modern age, I lose my confidence. I have no idea how to flirt or get a guy's attention at a bar or function. It's been more than twenty years since I've dated, and with this online dating stuff, the rules have dramatically changed.

One night at a party, I asked one of my single girlfriends, Jojo, how she manages to meet men. She said she has met men in all kinds of places, like the mall, the elevator, the grocery store... Wait—the elevator? You only have about ten seconds in an elevator, so how does that work? Instead of explaining, she goes into a detailed demonstration, role playing how she engages with a man in the elevator. It was impressive. Then she made me practice several times. It was hilarious as friends around us watched me pretend to talk to men in this imaginary elevator over and over. Jojo was pleased when I was able to demonstrate some level of mastery after many tries. But no matter how much "training" I have had, I still cannot muster up the courage to engage in a conversation with a man in the elevator. Thus, I have self-esteem and confidence, but I lack *situation-specific confidence*. If I wanted to say "Yes, I can talk to men in the elevator," I need to have confidence in my "approaching men" abilities. I need something known as self-efficacy.

Self-Efficacy

At one point, I worked as a career counselor at a local employment resource center. As an advocate for getting more women into the field of technology, I had secured funding through the Ontario Women's Directorate and created a ten-month technology program for women who had been out of the workforce for many years and living on social assistance. We focused on giving these women up-to-date career and life skills, the latest technology, and office skills—essentially everything they needed to know to get back into the workforce. I was thrilled to see that this program I had worked hard to create was producing the exact results I had hoped for: it was giving women a new outlook on their future and important tools they needed to support their families.

I remember one woman particularly well. I'll call her Susan. She was sweet and a very quick learner. She mastered the technology skills right away and spent her time helping the other women learn new skills. She was a great communicator. Everyone in the class liked her. I was excited when it came time to prepare her résumé because I knew it would be easy for her to find employment. So you can imagine my shock when Susan refused to send out her résumé.

We were in our final consultation before Susan was to leave for a three-month internship. Her résumé was beautifully typed and printed on crisp paper. Yet she flat-out refused to deliver her application to prospective employers.

"But why?" I asked.

Susan looked me straight in the eye and said, "What's the point? Even if I get the job, they're going to figure out right away that I'm an idiot and they'll fire me."

I was stunned. My star student had no idea how talented she was. It didn't matter that she learned quickly, taught the other women what they needed to know, and had excellent technology skills. She believed she was essentially useless. I realized then how powerful strongly held beliefs really are.

In this case, Susan had overall confidence, which she demonstrated by coming into the resource center every day. What she lacked was her belief that she could be successful if she started working in a real job. You see, that was a new domain for her, and self-efficacy is essentially situation-specific confidence; the science calls it "domain-specific." So while having overall confidence is a good thing, you need self-efficacy to give you the courage to act.

The Science of Saying Yes to What You Want

In July 2002, the American Psychological Association published a list of one hundred eminent psychologists of the twentieth century, and Canadian Dr. Albert Bandura was fourth on the list.[26] Dr. Bandura has been studying self-efficacy and what motivates people to act, and has contributed extensively to our understanding of how people think, behave, and feel.[27] When I first read Dr. Bandura's work on self-efficacy, I was so excited, I thought my head was going to pop off. His work enlightened me about why I was holding myself back in various areas of my life. I lovingly refer to the study of self-efficacy as the "science of saying yes to what you want," because once you raise your level of self-efficacy about what it is you really want, your thoughts, actions, and behaviors will all align with that goal.

According to Dr. Bandura, "perceived self-efficacy" refers to beliefs you have about whether you can successfully achieve certain goals. In other words, self-efficacy is our belief in our ability to be successful in a given situation—it is not whether you have the talent, skills, or resources to be successful. My student Susan had the skills and talent to be successful, but she didn't have the corresponding *belief* that she was skilled and talented and thus sabotaged her opportunities to find employment.

Science shows that we can increase our ability to achieve specific goals by managing our beliefs about ourselves, which drive our motivation. This can be the "juice" you need to muster the courage to say yes to your wants and desires. You might be scared out of your mind to ask for that promotion, but what will give you the courage to ask for it anyway? You might be hesitant to interview that big name for an article you're writing, but what will give you the mental boost to email her? You might be embarrassed to go to that dance class you love, so what will finally get you into those tights and onto the dance floor? Your beliefs about your competence in any given area fuel your motivation.

Beliefs Are Self-Fulfilling Prophecies

Our beliefs about whether we will be successful at achieving a certain goal play a big role in our motivation.

We begin with a belief about whether we will be successful if we engage in a certain task. For example, my friend Sheila would like to find her soulmate, but she has this belief: *I am overweight right now so no man will want to go out with me.* So when she goes to the grocery store she doesn't brush her hair or put on makeup and wears her schlumpy sweatpants. She doesn't even look at any men, because she doesn't believe any man would be interested in her. She never accepts my invitations to go out and meet single men; in fact, she never goes out. As a result, no men ask her out. Her interpretation of this result just reinforces her belief that no man will ever go out with her. Hence, her initial belief becomes a self-fulfilling prophecy.

Now let's take a look at another friend of mine. Brenda also wants to find her soulmate, and she is the same weight as Sheila, but her belief is *I am attractive at any weight.* When she goes to the grocery store, she always makes sure she looks good, because she never knows where she'll meet that special someone. She flirts with everyone she meets, wherever she goes. As a result, lots of men ask her out. Her interpretation of this result reinforces her belief that she is attractive to men. Hence, her initial belief becomes a self-fulfilling prophecy.

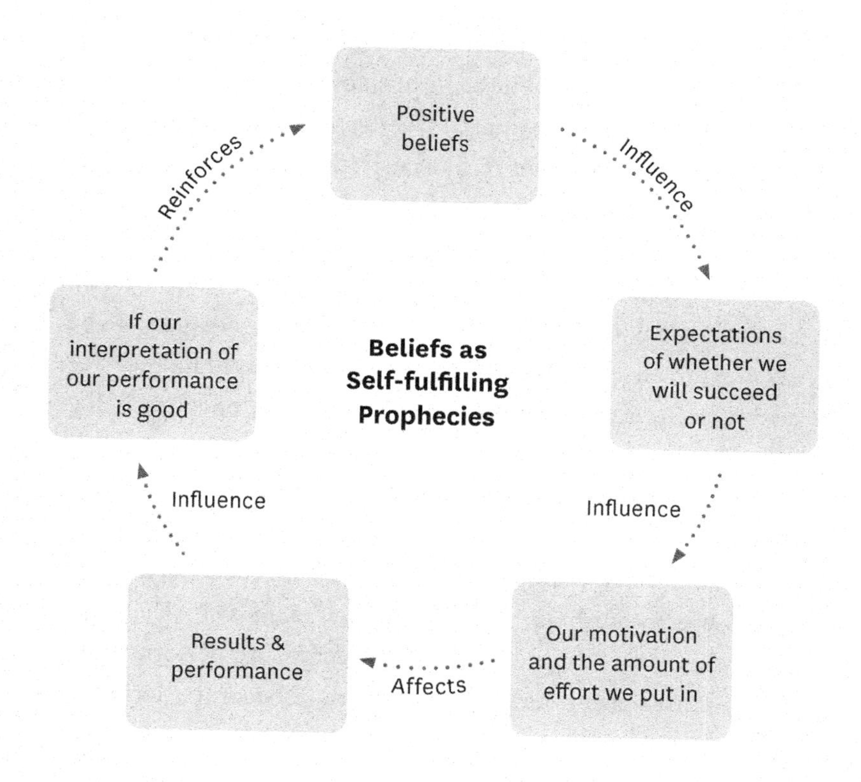

Scientists often refer to this scenario as the Pygmalion effect, also called the Rosenthal effect, created by Rosenthal and Jacobson.[28] Pygmalion is a character in Ovid's *Metamorphoses*, written in AD 8. Pygmalion is a sculptor who has had bad experiences with women and hates all of them. He has given up on finding love and instead fashions his perfect woman out of stone. Every day he speaks to the statue, caresses it, and lies down with it. He is in love. One day, Venus, the goddess of love, takes pity on Pygmalion and turns his statue into his perfect real woman. What he had envisioned becomes a self-fulfilling prophecy.

So it is true with our beliefs. If we believe we will see positive results or if we believe in our abilities, it is easy for us to muster the energy required to engage in the activities necessary to move us closer to our desired goals. Starting with a held belief motivates us to engage in certain behaviors or put a certain amount of effort into our performance, affecting the outcome. When we hold a preexisting belief that we will *not* be successful, we tend to not engage in the activities required to be successful, and when things do not go well, our brain receives a reinforcing message: *See? I told you so.* That negative belief grows stronger and that will affect future performances. Equally, if we have a preexisting belief that we *can* be successful, we are motivated to engage in success behaviors, increasing the likelihood of a stellar performance, and when we succeed, it sends a message to our brain: *See? I knew you could do it.* That positive belief grows stronger and will affect future performances. So we must master our beliefs if we are to become successful.

Shifting Beliefs

If people believe they have no power to produce a successful outcome, they typically will not act. If I'm expecting bad results, I'm typically running in the opposite direction—which might manifest as procrastination or self-sabotage. If we believe we will be successful, it is easier for us to jump right in. That's not to say that some very passionate people have not jumped right in, with no clue if they were going to be successful. These people have high self-efficacy in their ability to cope and deal with whatever comes their way. Self-efficacy is not a requirement for performance; it is a *factor* in performance, and people with high self-efficacy in a certain domain actually perform better and at higher levels.

Six Ways Self-Efficacy Contributes to Your Success

Through his research, Dr. Bandura found that people with high self-efficacy—that is, people with a strong belief in their capabilities to be successful—act, think, and feel differently from those with low self-efficacy. As a result, they can achieve higher levels of performance. If you want to perform better, take yourself to the next level, or play a bigger game, there are six reasons you'll want to increase your self-efficacy.

People high in self-efficacy:

1. Set Higher-Level Goals

People with high self-efficacy are more likely to set challenging goals for themselves and be more committed to the goal. When you believe in yourself and your capabilities, you start to see yourself in a new light. Once I believed that I was doing a good job delivering workshops, I started to believe that I could reach for a higher-level goal—keynote speaking. I had increased my self-efficacy around my speaking career. As my self-efficacy rises, so does my desire to continually set my sights higher and higher.

2. Expend More Effort toward Achieving Their Goals

People with high self-efficacy believe they will be successful if they keep trying, so they are more likely to push toward the finish line. High self-efficacy is motivating. Think about a time when you felt hopeless. You didn't believe that anything you could do would make a difference. How motivated were you to engage in the activities required to change things? Not very, I'm betting. Equally, believing that performing a certain set of actions will lead to a successful performance fuels our motivation to put in the effort required.

3. Persevere Longer in the Face of Adversity and Failure

Rather than giving up when the going gets tough, people with high self-efficacy show resilience. They see obstacles as challenges or new adventures, not threats. A challenge is something that you feel you have the chutzpah to overcome; if you fail miserably, you don't see how this failure could devastate you or ruin your reputation or lead to your demise. When tasks feel like threats, the opposite is true. The possible outcomes of your actions are sometimes so frightening that you stop yourself from trying. Self-efficacy allows you to see obstacles as challenges, which allows you to just keep persevering.

4. Bounce Back More Quickly

People with high self-efficacy speak to themselves more positively after a setback. Sometimes this internal dialogue can be a critical factor in our performance. Scientists have discovered that what you say to yourself after a poor performance can factor heavily into your ability to perform your best in your next performance. When your self-efficacy is high, you are naturally more optimistic about your abilities, which fuels your motivation to just get back up and try again.

5. Experience Less Stress

Efficacy beliefs also determine how much stress and depression we might experience in coping with difficult situations as we work hard toward our goals. When we feel confident about performing an upcoming task, we do not excessively worry about negative social evaluations, because we feel we will be successful at the task. When we are worrying less, we are stressing less.

6. Have Positive Outcome Expectancies

When people believe they will be successful in any given endeavor, they envision a positive outcome more readily. At a talk I gave at the University of Toronto, I asked the group of students what they felt most fearful about. One man raised his hand and said, "Public speaking." So I asked him what images he conjured when he thought about giving a speech. He responded, "I envision myself walking toward the podium, tripping, and falling flat on my face." No wonder he was fearful! Now that I have built my self-efficacy around speaking in public, I have visions of things going well (maybe because in all my years of speaking,

I have never once tripped on the way to the podium). I may still have concerns about how my talk will be received, but I do not have catastrophic visions about what might go wrong, which frees me of anxiety and fuels a better performance.

Self-Efficacy: The Key to Success

I hope you can see now how raising your self-efficacy in areas where you want to succeed can truly propel you to new levels. When Jack Canfield and Mark Victor Hansen came up with the idea of the Chicken Soup for the Soul series, they approached a few publishers, who told them their book was too lovey-dovey and that "nobody buys compilation books like that." Despite the negative feedback, Canfield and Hansen persevered, and were rejected by 144 publishers before one finally said yes. Over its lifetime, the Chicken Soup for the Soul series of books have sold over 500 million copies. Considering that in the United States the average book sells only 3,000 copies in its lifetime, that number is pretty astounding. When asked how they were able to persevere despite those rejections, Canfield says, "We had an unwavering belief in our idea."

When I reflect on this story, I realize that having a great idea is not enough for success. I mean, how many people would actually persevere through 144 rejections? Not many. So many organizations focus on increasing innovation without concurrent efforts to building employee self-efficacy. So many people I know have come up with great business ideas but didn't have the belief in their ideas to see them to fruition. That is why I believe that self-efficacy is critical for success.

Having a great idea is just the beginning. How many times have you had a brilliant idea for a new product or service and you don't do anything about it, and then a year later you learn that someone else built a very successful business around that idea? After the idea stage, you need to have the energy and motivation to bring it to life. You need to be ready to go after it and potentially defend your idea against the naysayers. The only way you will do that is by having an unwavering faith in your idea. That's what will take you to the finish line.

Sometimes envisioning a past success can be a great way to boost your self-efficacy. When we are reminded of times when we were successful in the past, it builds our self-efficacy and improves our confidence. Here's an exercise to instantly boost your confidence and bring to light the strengths you use when you are at your best. It's also a great exercise to do anytime you are feeling low on confidence.

EXERCISE: **YOU AT YOUR BEST**

1 Think of a time when you were flourishing at work. This could be something you did for an hour or a day, or something that took you several months to accomplish. It doesn't have to be anything monumental, it just has to be a time when you

felt you were doing an outstanding job and you were highly engaged and energized in your work—when you were thinking, *Wow, I am so good at what I do!* This could have been paid work or volunteer work or just a project you worked on.

2. Take five minutes to reflect on the following questions and write down the answers in a journal or on a blank sheet of paper.
   a. What was the situation?
   b. What were the conditions that allowed you to be at your best?
   c. What skills or strengths were you using?
   d. How did you feel? Why?
3. After reflecting on these questions, see if you can uncover the strengths that made you successful. Was it social intelligence? Perseverance? What strengths were you engaging in this scenario? Some strengths are more pronounced within a certain context, so by analyzing the conditions that allowed you to be your best, you start to determine the environments where you can more easily thrive. Knowing how your strengths flourish or are stifled under certain conditions can be an important factor in future performances.
4. Now share the story of when you were at your best with a trusted friend or colleague. Ask your friend to listen for the strengths you were using and to share them with you. Your friend's observations may bring you further insights into you

at your best. We call this strengths spotting. Compile a list of the strengths you observed in the story and those your friend observed.

5 Look at the strengths that made you successful. When you are aware of your strengths instead of focusing on your weaknesses, you are more likely to use them again. Focusing on strengths rather than weaknesses can be a powerful tool to boost your self-confidence because your focus is on what you can do rather than on what you can't do.

6 Reflect on this list of strengths and ask how you might engage those strengths in the future to boost the confidence you need to pursue your bigger goals.

Confidence Habits

- On your deathbed, you will regret more what you haven't done than what you've done. Identify the resources you need to get you past the fear of failure and decide to take one step toward your dreams.
- Focus less on self-esteem and more on increasing your self-efficacy in areas of your life where you want to take yourself to the next level.

- Beliefs can become self-fulfilling prophecies, so be aware of what your beliefs are and begin to shift them. (You'll learn more about how to do that in the chapters to come.)
- Get in the habit of analyzing your performance when things go well, so that you become familiar with the strengths that will take your competence to the next level.
- Engage in magical thinking for even greater strength.

5

Build Your Confidence Muscles

IF IT IS self-efficacy that gives us the courage to act, then we need to know how to build it if we are going to move into action joyfully. Remember, if we want to raise self-efficacy and wire our brain for confidence, we need to shift our beliefs. Here again I turn to the work of Dr. Albert Bandura, who has discovered that we formulate efficacy beliefs by interpreting information from four major sources.

1. Performance or Mastery Experiences

Successfully performing the task and attributing your success to your own efforts, skill, or knowledge is the most powerful source of self-efficacy, because if you believe you have accomplished the task successfully in the past, you are much more likely to believe you can do it again in the future. Merely performing the task is not enough—some people successfully perform the task but continually discount their success and so never change their self-belief about their competence levels.

Remember Susan, from the previous chapter? We knew she had the skills and knowledge to be successful, but her beliefs about her skills and knowledge stopped her from finding employment. Confidence is not about your talents, skills, and good looks. Confidence is about your *beliefs* about your talent, skills, and good looks. So it's not just about building competence, which is the first step; it is also about increasing your confidence in your competence. Let me tell you the rest of Susan's story.

I knew that Susan needed to go on her internship so that she could see for herself how good she was. I knew she needed to experience success and that this would change her perspective on things. Eventually, I persuaded her to do the internship. "Susan, this is a government internship," I said. "That means the employer doesn't pay one red cent to have you there. Even if you get there and all you can do is sweep the floor, they'll be happy you're there." Susan reluctantly accepted the position and off she went.

Over the next few months, reports from the employer were positive. She did well, and the employer was pleased with her work. I was hopeful she would return a new woman. The day came for Susan to return to the resource center. I sat her down and asked if she was ready to send out those résumés. "Louisa, I don't need to send out résumés. I already have a job."

I was stunned. "But how?"

"After a few days into my internship, I realized that I knew more than half the people who worked there—and I wasn't even getting paid! So about a month ago, I sent out a whole whack of résumés, and I found an office job for a small business near my home. Somehow you knew I needed to learn for myself that I could do the job. You were right." That was a glorious day. Dr. Bandura would call this a successful performance experience.

Susan had had several achievements in the past. She had successfully completed technical and administrative tasks in the comfort of our employment resource center, so why did this not change her beliefs about her abilities? She may have had one or more of the following beliefs:

- *I'm really only better than all the other women here because they've been out of the workforce for so many years. They are easy to beat.*

- *Louisa is my counselor, and she is just being nice to me to encourage me. Just wait until I get into a real work environment! Then they'll know I'm an impostor.*

- *The skills I'm learning here are different from the skills they will expect in a real job. I don't have those skills.*

Despite her successful skill-building experiences at the employment resource center, she did not believe in her abilities outside the center. Remember, efficacy beliefs are domain-specific, so you can see now how important it is to understand that your efficacy beliefs need to be laser-specific. It wasn't until Susan had an opportunity to actually compare her abilities with those of others that she finally replaced her limiting beliefs with new ones about her success. We are social creatures, and we seek social comparison all the time to see if our abilities are up to standard. How often do you unrealistically compare yourself to others and disqualify the positive accomplishments in your life? If you want to have successful performance experiences, you need to start seeing yourself with new eyes after every performance. Since this is the most powerful source of self-efficacy, I dedicate chapters 5 to 7 to techniques and strategies that will allow you to leverage your experiences for greater confidence.

2. Vicarious Experiences (aka Social Modeling)

Seeing people similar to ourselves succeed in certain endeavors increases our beliefs in our own capabilities in that area. There are two kinds of vicarious experiences: role modeling and mental rehearsal.

Role modeling

We are social creatures. Even as young as babies, human beings learn by watching others. Seeing others being successful at what we want to do can be a powerful influencer on our self-efficacy and can shift our beliefs from "No, I can't" to "Yes, I can." According to Dr. Bandura, role models can have a positive or negative effect on our self-efficacy, depending on how we perceive them.

Mental Rehearsal

People who visualize themselves delivering good performances and repeatedly mastering more challenging situations experience boosts in their self-efficacy. Neuroscientists have discovered that our brain sometimes cannot tell the difference between something we have experienced and something we have imagined. In one study, scientists wanted to know if the neurons in the brain responsible for vision were also activated during imagination.[29] They found an 88 percent overlap in the neurons that processed recalling seen information with those imagining the information. Tricking our minds into believing we have done something before is akin to having a performance experience, which increases self-efficacy. In chapter 8, I go into more detail about how you can effectively leverage role models and the best ways to practice mental rehearsal to boost self-efficacy and increase confidence.

3. Social Persuasion

Social persuasion involves others expressing faith in our capabilities and encouraging us with positive feedback. Don't underestimate the role social persuasion has on self-efficacy. Others telling us that we can do something can shift our beliefs and increase our self-efficacy. Equally, others telling us we can't do something decreases our self-efficacy. It is so important to surround yourself with positive, encouraging people when embarking on something new or big. I dedicate chapter 9 to how you can effectively leverage those around you to increase your self-efficacy.

4. Bodily and Emotional States

Our body sends certain messages to the brain that, depending on how we interpret these messages, can either increase or decrease self-efficacy. Our body postures, our physical activity, and our perceived body image can all factor into our feelings of confidence. Also, we often base our judgments about our level of confidence by the emotions we experience when we think about performing an upcoming task, so understanding those emotional triggers is also important. Dr. Bandura has discovered that people in a depressed mood have lowered efficacy beliefs, which may lead to lowered motivation. Most people I speak with are surprised to hear about the extent to which the body contributes to feelings of confidence, but it's an area that should not be overlooked. I dedicate chapter 10 to tools and techniques that are important for managing your bodily and emotional states to improve confidence.

Now that we know the four major sources of self-efficacy, let's explore each in greater detail, so that we know how we can use each to wire our brain for confidence.

Performance or Mastery Experiences

When people ask me what is the best way to reduce self-doubt and increase the courage to act, I tell them that it's to go out and try the task in question, and then to try it again. Building your competence will chip away at your self-doubt, replacing it with feelings of confidence. Remember my story about going to dance class? After several classes, my confidence rose and my self-doubt disappeared. Typically, people stop themselves from trying new things because they do not want to fail in front of others. The potential embarrassment acts as a deterrent. One way to increase your courage to act, then, is to make it safe to fail.

Make It Safe to Fail

Let's go back again to Susan's story. I offered Susan a "low likelihood of failure" experience by sending her on an internship. Not only was it a job I found for her but the employer wasn't paying and knew she was a beginner—I had managed the employer's expectations. I call this scenario a nonthreatening baby step toward full employment somewhere. Remember, it's important to have performance experiences that are successful if you want to increase your self-efficacy.

When I was completing my master's degree, I had to deliver a final project (known as a capstone project), which was to be an application of what I had learned in taking my degree. I completed this project with my dear friend and colleague Shannon Polly. We decided that we would create four workshops in positive psychology and pilot them with four of my existing corporate clients. Then we would write up the results. Because it was the first time we had ever delivered positive psychology workshops, they were not perfect, and we learned so much about what *not* to do. But by setting up a pilot, we gave ourselves permission to be imperfect. It was a safe place to fail. Our clients knew it was all untested and agreed to participate. Incorporating a pilot into our capstone project increased our confidence about delivering workshops in positive psychology and gave us valuable feedback, which we used to improve the workshops. Now the workshops are highly successful and popular. Pilots are good ways to take a safe risk.

James Dyson, the billionaire entrepreneur and inventor of the bagless vacuum cleaner, makes failure an expected part of inventing new designs. He is the poster boy for failure, with 5,127 failed attempts before succeeding with the winning prototype of a bagless vacuum cleaner. At the Dyson Corporation, he creates a supportive work environment by removing criticism and encouraging a culture that is constantly learning from its mistakes. "Failure is a wonderful starting point because when something fails, you know exactly what the problem is, and you have to think and experiment to overcome that failure," says Dyson.[30] This is a critical success factor for the company. He expects failure and, as a result, he continues to foster great innovation within his engineering team. Dyson makes it safe to fail.

Set Mini Learning Goals

Goal-setting research confirms that setting *performance* goals actually increases performance, except in the case when someone is learning something new. If I do not know anything about how I am going to go about achieving a certain goal and I nevertheless set a performance goal for myself, this may cause me some stress, as I do not know the steps necessary to be successful. I can't see how I am going to get from here to there. Scientists have discovered that when we are learning something new, it is best to set several preliminary *learning* goals, which must be achieved in order to move successfully toward achieving the final goal. For example, for many years, "Publish a book" was on my goals list, but I had no clue how to publish a book, so I remained unmotivated.

Then in the summer of 2013, I received a phone call from book marketing coach Geoff Affleck, who works with Marci Shimoff (bestselling author of *Happy for No Reason* and *Chicken Soup for the Woman's Soul*), and Janet Bray Attwood and Chris Attwood (bestselling authors of *The Passion Test*). They were offering a four-day mastermind retreat in San Francisco for people who wanted to publish a book. I decided this was exactly what I needed to get started on my life-long dream of becoming a bestselling author. We spent the four days learning how to write and publish a bestselling book. Now I knew all the mini-goals I had to achieve in order to move toward publishing a book. It wasn't about just starting to write, it was about *learning* how to get a book published that got me into action.

Think about anything you are fearful of doing but that you really want to do. Then consider what mini learning goals or goals you might set to help you achieve this goal. Maybe you are afraid to confront a loved one or a coworker about their behavior and how it is negatively affecting you. Taking a course on "how to have a difficult conversation" might improve your confidence in this area, so that you can enter into the discussion with more ease. Maybe you are dating again for the first time in twenty years. A dating coach might teach you more about dating successfully and make the process more enjoyable. (And when you finally discover how to make dating in your fifties more enjoyable, please call me and tell me how!) Maybe you're afraid to ask for a promotion. Speaking to a colleague about how they did it or finding resources on the Web might be a good start. When you know nothing about how to start, get focused on learning, and break down the big goal into manageable mini learning goals.

Take Baby Steps

Sometimes it is less about learning and more about going out and actually doing it. In these situations, it's easier to take one small step at a time. Think about a big goal you have for yourself. Now think about ten baby steps toward that goal. For example, if writing a book is a dream of yours but also a scary prospect, here are ten baby steps you could take:

1. Ghostwrite a blog post for a friend if you don't want your name out there just yet. See how the post is received. Are you getting some interesting comments and feedback? If you feel comfortable, then...
2. Be a guest blogger for a friend or colleague and put your byline on the post. How did that go? Are you more comfortable

now with people commenting on your writing? If you feel good about that, then...

3. Ask other friends and colleagues if you could be a guest blogger for them. Get comfortable with a few of these, then...
4. Write a short newsletter and send it out to just friends and family. Then...
5. Begin writing your own blog. Now you can see which posts your audience likes and which ones they don't like so much. Each blog is an opportunity for learning. Then...
6. Reach out to your favorite publications and ask if you might write an article for them. Then...
7. Ask to write articles for your favorite magazines. Then...
8. Seek out an opportunity to contribute a chapter for a compilation book. Then...
9. Write an ebook and give it away. See what kind of response you get.
10. If all that goes well, now maybe you won't be so afraid to begin writing your own printed and bound book... so start writing!

The key to taking baby steps is to set yourself up to successfully achieve each step, thereby increasing your feelings of competence after every step. Trying something and failing miserably may lower your self-efficacy beliefs. So perhaps before you post a blog entry, have a trusted colleague edit it and give you feedback. Maybe you can hire a writing coach to help you through each step, continuing to learn as you progress. With each successful baby step, you will build your competence, which will boost your confidence and shift your belief to "Yes, I can do this."

At the beginning, it will be important to take criticism with a grain of salt. If you are new at something, accept that you might not be so perfect and that people may criticize you. Better yet, expect it. Say to yourself, *Yes, I know it's not perfect. This is all new. I'm not there yet.* It is a lot easier to deal with criticism when you're expecting it than when you're not expecting it. It will soften the blow. So often people try things, get shut down, and never try again. Don't ever allow yourself to fall into that trap.

Increase Optimism

Sometimes in order for us to begin, we need to change our outlook from one of pessimism to one of optimism. If we are pessimistic about our expected outcomes, we may feel hopeless and never get started on the journey of achieving our big goals. Some people believe that we're either born optimistic or we're not. Research tells us otherwise.

Dr. Martin Seligman, the founding father of positive psychology, has spent decades studying optimism and has discovered that optimism can be learned. One difference between optimists and pessimists is what he calls their *explanatory style*.[31] Explanatory style is one's learned and habitual way of explaining bad events or situations in one's life. This could be a habit you learned in childhood or adolescence, and it determines whether you feel hopeful or helpless. Training our brain to have an optimistic explanatory style can move us powerfully forward. In his research, Seligman determined three components of explanatory style.

1. Explaining a Bad Event as Something Permanent in Your Life, or as Something Temporary

When we see negative circumstances in our lives as a permanent way of being, and that things are never going to change, we adopt a pessimistic view. If we feel there is nothing we can do to change the situation, we'll do nothing about it. We will feel hopeless. But when we can see circumstances as temporary, we are hopeful that the situation will be different in the future and we'll try again. Thus, how we project today's events into the future affects us going forward.

For example, one of my friends, a single woman in her thirties, commented that she was not good with financial matters: "You know me and money, Louisa. We just don't go together." She saw her financial situation as something that was never going to change—she would forever struggle with it. I explained to her that she needed to take responsibility for her finances, because no one else was stepping up to take care of them for her. If she didn't, who would? Soon after, she hired a financial planner, who showed her how to take care of her finances and how to save for her future. She saved her money, began paying off her debt, and after only one year found herself in such a healthy financial situation that she could go on that

Caribbean vacation she so desired. Once she was able to change the label she had placed on herself—"bad with money"—she realized that she was able to increase her financial savviness and so was able to change.

My friend had given herself a label she felt was permanent. Once we peeled off that label, she was able to move in the right direction. Do you label yourself a nonexerciser, bad at math, unlucky? What if you labeled yourself with a positive label like "daily exerciser," "good at math," and "a lucky person." You would be surprised at the mental shift that can take place just by replacing a pessimistic belief with a more optimistic one.

But sometimes it is not about the label. Sometimes we get so stuck in a belief that we don't explore the information necessary to change our situation. A close friend was living with a man who, she felt, was overbearing and toxic. She is absolutely gorgeous, intelligent, and fun to be around, so why on earth would she not leave him to be with someone who treated her right? "I could never afford the mortgage without him" was her response. I asked her a very useful question.

"Is that true?"

"Of course it's true."

"I mean, have you gone to the bank, figured out how much your mortgage payments would go up if you paid him out, and asked the bank if there is anything you can do to stretch out the payments so that you could manage without him?"

"No, I haven't done that."

"Well, until you figure that part out, you'll never really know." Then we changed the topic.

The next day she called me. "I kicked him out."

"You did? But what about the mortgage?"

"I met with my accountant this morning and, with a few changes, I can easily manage the mortgage without him."

Sometimes we are so stuck in our beliefs that we stop seeking new information, information that might turn a seemingly hopeless situation into a hopeful one.

One way to know if you are engaging in "permanent" thinking about your current situation is to be on the lookout for how often you use the words "never" and "always." If you are saying to yourself, "I will never be an entrepreneur" or "I will always be alone" or "I will never be able to exercise every day" or "I will never [insert your dream here]," how will you move toward those goals? When you label yourself a certain type of person ("I've been ten pounds heavier than I should be, my whole life") you limit yourself to your current reality. If you are using the word "never," ask yourself how things could be different. If you are using the word "always," ask yourself about a time when it wasn't like this. When we find the exception, even just one, we can open ourselves to new possibilities.

2. Seeing the Situation as Pervasive or Specific

When we experience a problem or are in the midst of a situation, we can either see it as all encompassing, affecting every aspect of our life, or as specific. One day, my daughter received a poor score on her science test. "I'm such a bad student," she said. I reminded her that she is actually an excellent student—in fact, top of her class for many years running. She just didn't do as well on that particular test. I was helping her see that her poor score was specific to that test and did not encompass every course she was taking.

I spent ten years working with corporate transition organizations. Companies looking to downsize would come to us to help their laid-off employees find new jobs. Some people were so distraught about losing their job, they felt depressed and anxious most of the time. They could not see that the layoff affected only one domain of their life—their career. Instead, they saw themselves as failures as a spouse and parent, they were embarrassed to let their friends know about their layoff, and they stopped exercising and let themselves eat whatever they wanted to soothe the pain of it all. They were allowing one specific domain of their life to become pervasive and ruin the enjoyment of every other domain.

Once again, a very effective question to stop us from blowing a situation out of proportion is to ask ourselves, *Is it true?* When a friend says, "No man will ever love me," I ask her, "Is that true? Because you were engaged just a few months ago and you have always had boyfriends in the past. Just because this one relationship didn't work out doesn't mean you won't have another relationship in the future." By focusing on just one specific aspect, you can maintain your good feelings about everything else that is going on in your life.

3. Seeing a Bad Event as Being Caused by You Personally, or by Someone Else

I was on a bus one day and the driver was angry. As the bus filled to capacity she started to kick people off the bus by yelling,

"Shoo, shoo!" Then she began yelling at the people who were standing ahead of the white line near the front door—the line you're supposed to stand *behind*. As people got on and off the bus, she continued to yell and call people names. I finally could not stand it anymore and said to her, "Please stop yelling at people; they are just doing their best to fit on the bus."

Well, she turned her wrath on me, calling me names and saying that I obviously was a person who had no sympathy for bus drivers and didn't care that I was treating her poorly. I ignored her comments, as I could see she was just an angry old battle ax. As I turned to the door to get off at my stop, she yelled, "Oh good, the bitch is getting off my bus!" The entire episode was shocking. I had never encountered an employee so rude in my thirty years of taking public transit in Toronto. I wrote a letter to the transit commission, suggesting this poor woman be given anger management training. The point I'm trying to make here is I didn't take it personally. She was insulting me, so I could have, but I am able to recognize other people's garbage when it comes my way.

When you take things personally, you believe you are the cause of the negative external event when, in fact, you were not responsible for it at all. Has this happened to you? It's a hard one to overcome, especially in business. Often decisions get made for business or financial reasons that are out of our control, and yet we constantly think that they are all about us. I observed in my work in corporate transition that even when a large group of employees were let go, there was always a handful of them who were convinced there was something wrong with them. "Why would they let the top performers go?" they'd say. "I must have been a bottom performer." Even in the midst of a huge downsizing in which hundreds of people were let go, they took it personally.

Often when we personalize, we incorporate our beliefs about what has happened into our self-concept without even finding out if it's true. If your boss hasn't explicitly said you were a bottom performer, you don't know anything for sure. Now, let's say your boss *did* say that you were one of the bottom performers. And if your boss thinks you are a bottom performer, that must mean you *are* a bottom performer, right? Wrong. In reality, the only thing you now know for sure is that your boss's *perception* of your performance was that it was bad. I have seen time and again people who are star performers—doing well for years on end, getting promotions and bonuses each year—get fired when a new boss comes in, because of that new boss's *perception*.

I'm not saying you shouldn't listen to feedback or ask yourself if there is something you could have done differently. I'm just saying don't let that feedback *define* you. You need to depersonalize it. Learn what you can about the experience and how you can improve in the future and stop making it all about you all the time. People with high self-efficacy will attribute their failure to poor planning or low effort, rather than to a lack of ability. Thus, they are more likely to seek out new strategies to help improve in future performances. In other words, when you don't take things personally, you are more likely to just get back up and keep trying.

Everything is figure-out-able.

MARIE FORLEO

Recapping Optimism

By seeing situations as more temporary, specific, and impersonal, you can increase your optimism and your courage to act. This higher level of optimism will allow you to more easily focus on improving your competence, thereby boosting your confidence. And remember, one of the best tools to flip pessimism into optimism is to ask yourself, *Is it true?* You will be surprised how quickly that can shift your beliefs toward a more optimistic way of thinking when you are feeling particularly hopeless about a certain situation.

Making it safe to fail, setting mini-goals, taking baby steps, and increasing optimism are all good ways to increase your courage to act. Once you get into action, you'll want to slowly build your feelings of competence for higher and higher levels of confidence. Here are some strategies to help build your competence.

Deliberate Practice

Getting better at something does not mean just practicing the same thing over and over—as yoga instructor Chuck Miller says, "Practice makes permanent." Just because I go to yoga every day doesn't mean I am able to perform tricky balancing poses or a headstand. I just go and enjoy my class. I have friends who can do all those fancy moves because they work hard at advancing their skills. According to Anders Ericsson, psychologist and researcher at Florida State University, and his colleagues, becoming an expert at something does not take just practice, it takes *deliberate practice*: consistently and deliberately improving your performance every time.[32] If you want to reach higher and higher levels of competence, you need to be deliberate about what you want to learn in each baby step and set up the experience accordingly. For example, I have been a speaker for many years, but I wanted to take my skills to an even higher level, so I hired a speaking coach to work with me. After my coach hears me speak, she offers her feedback and gives me something to work on next. This allows me to focus on certain skills I can improve upon. Some people feel uncomfortable analyzing their performance or hearing feedback, but if you want to improve in that area, you have to be open to feedback. It's not enough just to practice. You really have to focus on how you will improve each try.

Know What Conditions Make You Successful

Understand that you won't always shine in certain environments. Your talents and strengths might be wonderful, but sometimes we are top of our game in one environment and fail miserably in another environment. "Weaknesses" sometimes are simply strengths out of context. So it is important to not only reflect on your performance but also on the *conditions* under which you were successful.

I was once asked to give a thirty-minute talk at a breakfast meeting of fifteen CEOs. I thought it was a fabulous marketing opportunity, so I agreed. The talk went amazingly well, with several of the CEOs calling me to do work with their organizations. I scratched my head, wondering what was different about this talk that made it so successful. So I analyzed the conditions:

- It was first thing in the morning.
- The CEOs were mostly female.
- The topic was business performance.
- The CEOs loved hearing about the science behind what I was talking about.

Equipped with this information, I can now set myself up for greater success in the future: I can target the audiences where my message will be well received, and set up conditions for optimal performance. I know my message resonates most with a female audience, so I investigated which industries are female-dominated—public relations and fashion retailers, for instance—so that I can target them with my business marketing. If I have a choice, I schedule my talk for first thing in the morning, when I have the most energy. I always highlight the research behind my tools and strategies when speaking, as that increases my credibility.

We may feel bad when our performance does not go as planned, without ever thinking about our winning context. When things don't go well, can you depersonalize the situation and ask yourself what conditions would have helped you perform better? Make sure you have all the information. The "You at Your Best" exercise in chapter 4 is a great tool for exploring the conditions that put you in the best light.

Reflect More When Things Go Well

Another way to build self-efficacy is to take responsibility for your successes. When things go wrong, we are all too quick to call everyone into the boardroom for a full debrief, which usually involves a lot of finger pointing. Everyone is on the defensive as they desperately try to prove their worth. But how often have you debriefed when things have gone unexpectedly well? I have asked this question to thousands of people in my workshops and trust me, no hands ever go up!

I mentioned that the year my colleagues and I founded the CPPA, we decided to hold a big conference. Not only did we not yet have a dime to our name but we didn't even have a company bank account, website, or one member apart from the founders. But the conference was a huge success. We made the numbers we wanted to make (which were highly optimistic), and we had amazing feedback from conference attendees, including that it "was the best conference they had ever attended." I had never organized a conference before and, looking back on it, I wondered, *How did we do that?* So we created a survey asking our team about every aspect of the conference planning. We wanted to document what made us successful so we could recreate it at our next conference in two years' time. Shortly after our second conference, a colleague said to me, "I thought there was no way we were going to be able to top that first conference, but I believe we just did!"

Get in the habit of analyzing your greatest successes and you'll discover information different from what you would by just analyzing when things go wrong. Use that information to help you take your individual or company performance to the next level. Knowing what works and acknowledging how you contributed personally to your successful outcome is a necessary step in building your self-efficacy.

Take the Focus off Yourself

Often we are thinking about how we look, how we feel, and what people are thinking about us rather than focusing on the task at hand. I have been delivering workshops for fifteen years and feel quite comfortable doing so. But every once in a while I get nervous about a new group or a new topic, or about speaking in front of a group I believe is skeptical. It's usually because I am so focused on my delivery. I think, *What if they ask me a question I can't answer?* or *What if they don't like my topics and think it's all stupid?*

When I shift focus from myself to my audience, I calm down. I think about how I can effectively share my knowledge with the people in the room. I reassure myself that this group asked me to deliver the workshop for a reason—that I have something of value to share with their group. So if I am feeling a little nervous before a speaking engagement, I ask myself, *How can I best serve everyone in the room? How can I best love everyone in the room?* If I contemplate that, I end up doing a much better job. And if there is a question I can't answer, I say, "I'll get back to you with the answer." If there are people who don't like the workshop, that's okay. Usually the majority love it and one or two participants may not be fully satisfied. You'll never please everyone. When you are trying new things, think about how much more effective you will be at helping others, delivering your message, or reaching that end goal if you focus more on serving others rather than on yourself.

Recalling Past Performance Experiences to Increase Self-Efficacy

When I am working with people who are low in confidence about an upcoming event, I ask them a set of solution-focused questions that jog their memory about when they have been successful in that particular endeavor in the past. These questions are specifically designed to increase self-efficacy because they get people thinking about previous successes. Often people forget they have already achieved a certain amount of success even in areas where they are feeling low in confidence. We know that performance experiences increase self-efficacy; recalling them can also increase self-efficacy. Most people report a quick shift upward in positive mental energy and confidence after answering these questions.

EXERCISE: **CONFIDENCE-BUILDING SOLUTION-FOCUSED QUESTIONS**

Is there something in your life you would really like to do next, but you are not feeling confident about it, so you avoid it? Do you have something coming up in your life that you are anxious about, and you want to raise your level of confidence about it? Next time you are feeling particularly low in confidence about something you need to undertake, ask yourself these questions. (Or ask a trusted colleague to ask you them.)

1. First, recall a time when you were successful at doing that particular thing in the past (or doing something similar). Then ask yourself: What was key to my success? What did I do then that made me successful? How did I manage to do that? What is one thing I did then that I am not doing now?
2. Considering what I am embarking on now, what is already going well? What small successes have I had so far?
3. How can I do more of what is already going well?
4. How have I managed to get this far?
5. What does that tell me about myself?
6. What have I done in the past that might help me now?
7. What personal qualities and strengths do I have that will help me be successful?
8. What ideas do I have for solving this?
9. Who can help me with this?
10. Who would have a different perspective on this?

Take some time with these questions and try to recall your past performance experiences. When you realize you have done this same endeavor successfully in the past, you will quickly shift into believing you can do it again. If you haven't done exactly the same thing, contemplate similar parts of the experience that you mastered in the past. (For example, many years ago, I was asked to deliver my first ever keynote address. I had already delivered numerous workshops, but never a keynote. I was not feeling confident about it. After asking myself the questions above, I realized that I had actually mastered many keynote skills in all my years of workshop delivery. Taking the leap to keynote deliveries no longer seemed as daunting. I worked on the gaps to improve my skills and my confidence shot up again.) The other questions also get you thinking about the progress you have already made with this accomplishment, rather than your shortcomings. This gets you thinking about everything that is already working in your favor, and you will experience a boost in confidence.

Once you have asked yourself the questions above and are feeling a shift in your confidence, ask yourself this important question:

What is one small step I can take to get myself closer to my goal?

Commit to taking that step.

Source: Haesun Moon and Simon Lee, Solution-Focused Brief Coaching.

Confidence Habits

- Engage in performance experiences that will allow you to improve your competence in achieving your big goals.
- Set mini learning goals and decide on the baby steps you will take toward your goals.
- Increase your optimism about achieving your big goals by seeing setbacks as temporary, specific, and nonpersonal.
- Don't just analyze what happened when things go wrong. Take the time to analyze when things go well, to learn from your successes.
- Engage in deliberate practice, to take your skills to higher levels every try.
- Ask yourself solution-focused, confidence-building questions that recall past performance experiences. These memories will boost your feelings of competence and confidence. Focus on what is already working for you.

What to Do When You Fall

YOU'VE DECIDED to find the courage and take steps toward your bigger goals. Great! So we embark on this new journey and we believe that our success should increase slowly and steadily, like this:

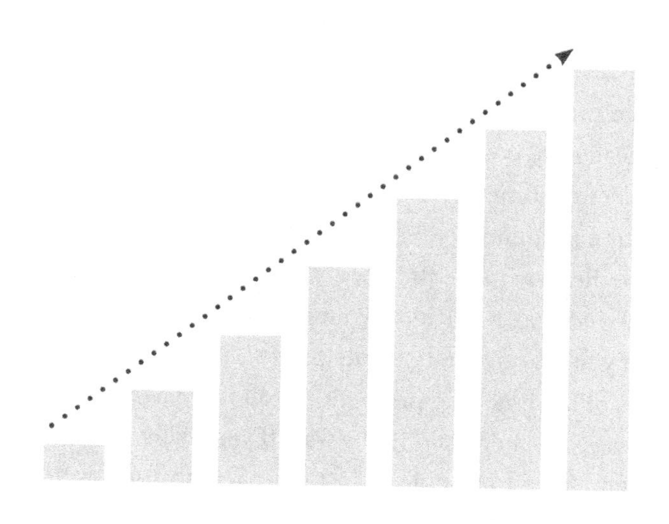

But success is messy and in reality looks much more like this:

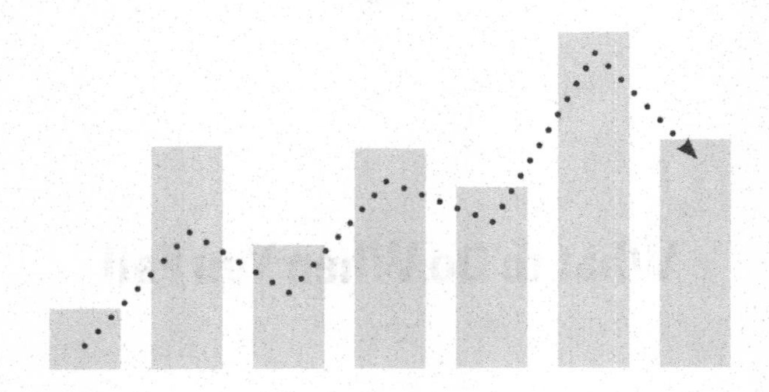

Things do not always go as planned. Along the way, you may fail or be disappointed with your performance. When you're pushing the envelope, you're going to stumble. At the beginning of starting something new, your confidence will be weak. Failure may deter you from moving forward or cause you to give up all together. So you need to be prepared for it. As you become more competent by doing, you need to be ready to realistically and constructively navigate your successes and your setbacks for ultimate learning, while maintaining and increasing your confidence.

Whether you move the needle on your self-efficacy depends mainly on what you say to yourself after each attempt, especially if you are going after some pretty big goals, like losing fifty pounds or landing a big promotion. You may have some success and disappointments along the way. If you really want what you want, you have to be able to just get back up after every disappointment and keep going.

I went through a particularly rough time once when working with the CPPA. I thought it was the end. Every morning, I dreaded getting out of bed. I felt like I was buried under six feet of mud. But I would picture myself putting on my waders—like the rubber overalls fly-fishers wear—and I would pull myself out of bed and get right back in the mud and keep on trudging.

I wish I could tell you it will all be smooth sailing, but I would be lying. There will be days when you will think that everybody hates you. But that's when you have to say, so what? You can't control everything, especially others' reactions. Nor can you expend all your energy trying to control the situation.

It is not our failure that matters; it is our recovery. What is truly important is what you say to yourself after the fact. The substance of your self-talk will determine if this experience will increase your self-efficacy, reduce your self-efficacy, or keep it at the existing level.

Master Your Self-Talk

Completely mastering those voices in your head to be performance enhancing, rather than deflating, takes time and a lot of practice. If after every setback your self-talk is horribly critical, your confidence will suffer and the positive mental energy you need in order to try again will be zapped. Unfortunately, that appears to be the default for most people. Everywhere I go, people tell me how hard they are on themselves. On the other hand, if your self-talk is always light and fluffy and positive, you may not be opening yourself to learning and growth.

If you want to build your confidence after each new learning event, aim for *constructive* self-talk—whether that be positive or negative. Aha! You thought that your self-talk always had to be positive, didn't you? Let me show you how you might look critically at a past failure with a constructive and energizing approach.

A number of years ago, I missed a speaking engagement. Obviously, when someone asks you to speak and people are showing up to hear you speak, it is a disaster to just not show up. It can absolutely hurt your reputation. I had been asked to speak at a one-day conference, and mine was the opening keynote address. It was on my calendar for 9:30 a.m., so I was planning my arrival for 9 a.m., which would give me plenty of time to prepare. On that particular day, the traffic was horrendous, and even though I left myself plenty of time, I found myself running late. I arrived at 9:10, still in time to get into action. The problem was that my presentation was actually scheduled for 9 a.m.! When I went back to check my emails, they indeed said 9 a.m. It was obvious that the organizers were disappointed in me. Luckily for me, a friend who was scheduled to do the closing keynote address took my place and I did the closing keynote instead. But I was still distraught over my unprofessional conduct.

Here are two options for self-talk in such a scenario.

Option 1: Beat Yourself Up (and Be Horribly Critical)

I'm such an idiot. I can't believe my life is so out of control and disorganized. What is wrong with me? Embarrassing. What are people going to think of me? Not much of a keynote speaker! Feelings of shame and embarrassment filled my body.

It is important to understand the kind of impact this self-talk has on me and my upcoming performance.

1. First, how does it make me feel as a speaker? Am I feeling good about my skills or talents? Definitely not. So I am allowing an emotional drain here.
2. Second, I want to analyze the effects this self-talk has on my "next behaviors." That is, does this self-talk energize me to get back up and keep persevering, or does it zap my energy and send me down the highway of depression? Catastrophizing about the worst-case scenario is a good way to zap my energy and possibly derail my upcoming performance.
3. Third, how does this self-talk affect my learning? If I want to get better at something, I need to find learning in my successes and our failures. Not much learning here.

As you can see, beating up on yourself is not helpful if you want to improve your performance and try again. We may feel that we need to be hard on ourselves in order to improve, but that is not the case. This kind of self-talk, by the way, can also lead to depression and anxiety. Let's try again.

Option 2: Be Constructively Critical without the Beating-Up Part

Wow! I am so grateful my friend was there to do the opening address. Luckily for me, people in the audience didn't even know the difference. Practicing gratitude and curiosity are great tools to move you away from beating yourself up and toward a constructive way of learning from your setbacks. I often use gratitude to bounce back—and there is *always* something to feel grateful about. Here, I reminded myself that things might have been worse and that I'm grateful they weren't. Next, it is time to get curious with these questions:

1. What is this experience telling me? What did I learn from it? *That with every speaking engagement, I need to have an engagement contract that outlines all the details, for me to refer to. This will keep me more organized.*

2. How would I do things differently next time? *I will confirm all the speaking details at least a week in advance.*

3. What exactly went wrong? *This is a sign that my business is growing and I need help. There is nothing wrong with me; this can happen when I have just too much on my plate. Maybe it is time to hire an assistant. I have always had one in the past. My plan is to look into this. Also, give myself more time to get to the location.*

4. What parts of it did I get right? *Prepping my presentations well in advance served me well this time. As I was somewhat thrown off my game, being prepared helped me stay calm. (I will ensure I continue to do that.)*

5. What conditions contributed to this failure? *I have too much on my plate. Either hire an assistant or start cutting back.*

6 Who can I call to help me figure this out? *I think I have it. Don't overthink it—be so happy and grateful that everything turned out fine! Go and deliver the best talk ever!*

Can you see the difference when you speak to yourself constructively?

1 First, how does this banter make me feel as a speaker? Am I feeling good about my skills and talent? Yes, because what happened was not about my speaking: I am directing my analysis to my organizational skills and keeping it specific.

2 Second, I want to analyze the effects this self-talk has on my "next behaviors." This kind of self-talk does not zap my energy and allows me to maintain my positive energy for a good talk.

3 Third, how does this self-talk affect my learning? I learned a lot from this experience! In fact, shortly afterward, I hired an administrative assistant.

Let me tell you how this story ended. My talk went amazingly well. In fact, the organizers thought that my talk was a better message for the end of the day and that the switched order benefited everyone. I have not missed a talk since. Not even been late. I won't lie, it took some time for the sting I felt every time I thought about this screw-up to go away, but now I see it as an important learning experience.

Option 2 is what I call "positively and negatively constructive." I identify where I went wrong and what I need to fix, and I identify what helped save me and reinforce that I have some good habits. You will also notice that I did not focus on attacking me as a person—rather, I focused on analyzing only the task at hand. That allows me to maintain my self-esteem in a bad situation. Can you see how much more helpful this kind of self-talk is than all-negative self-talk?

What do you say to yourself after a setback? Let's look at common thinking traps we may fall into, and how we can turn them around to be more helpful and performance enhancing.

Self-Talk

Aaron Beck, commonly known as the founder of cognitive behavioral therapy, identified several patterns of thinking that lead to depression and anxiety and that could also contribute to self-doubt and a lack of confidence. Cognitive behavioral therapy is based on the idea that critical or automatic negative thoughts (ANTs) exaggerate situations, resulting in emotional disorders. Psychologists have identified a number of thinking traps people commonly fall into that can block us from having the realistic beliefs required to be successful. Here I want to identify how these dysfunctional ways of thinking can reduce self-efficacy or beliefs in your ability to succeed. See if you engage in any of these thinking traps. I have engaged in every single one! We'll also explore how you can shift out of these thinking traps to more helpful ways of thinking.

First, the list, before we get into the discussion:

- Seeing things through a negative lens → Being realistic
- Black-and-white thinking → Allowing imperfection
- Impostor phenomenon → Taking ownership of success
- Being psychic → Checking for the truth
- Predicting the future → Being open to new outcomes
- Catastrophizing → Seeing opportunities

Seeing Things through a Negative Lens → Being Realistic

You fixate on one single negative detail about a situation and see it only through that negative lens; you are incapable of realistically analyzing your performance.

At the end of every workshop I deliver, I ask people to fill out an evaluation form. I used to dread getting them back and reading the criticisms people had of my work. If I got forty-eight stellar reviews and two bad reviews, I would fixate on the two that were bad. Not only that, those two would overpower the other forty-eight, and I would believe that the workshop had been terrible. And my then husband would say, "Why do you always focus on the two bad workshop reviews when the other forty-eight are amazing?"

Do you do this to yourself? If so, you may be robbing yourself of opportunities to build your self-confidence about your abilities. This is when understanding the neuroscience can be helpful.

Understand Your Negativity Bias

Psychologists have discovered that the human brain has evolved with what is known as a "negativity bias." Negative events such as unpleasant thoughts, social interactions, or adverse situations have a greater impact on our psychological state than do neutral or positive events. Researchers hypothesize that, in prehistoric days, we were constantly looking for threats, which protected us from being attacked or eaten by predators. Since those ancient parts of our brain still exist, our brain is continually looking for the bad. As soon as it finds it, it fixates on it with tunnel vision. You see, if you were a caveperson and walked right by a strawberry patch without noticing it, you might go hungry that night. But if you strolled right by a saber-toothed tiger without noticing it, you would be dead. This is why we feel the *bad* so much stronger than the *good*.[33] We are hardwired to focus on the negative, and we tend to overestimate threats or criticism. It is no wonder one negative event among many positives can influence the filter through which we see the world.

One thing to help shift your negativity filter toward a more realistic view is to be mindful of the degree to which our brain is wired to focus on the bad. Then realistically look at the feedback or the particular situation and see if you can properly assess how much of it was actually bad. For example, over time, I learned how to be more realistic about my workshop feedback. Forty-eight great evaluations out of fifty puts the great evaluations at 96 percent, which is very high. Now, if twenty-five out of fifty were bad, I would know the workshop needed improving. But 96 percent is actually outstanding and requires little work to improve. If you are stuck, ask for feedback from your peers. Sometimes others can see more objectively than you can.

It is impossible to live without failing at something, unless you live so cautiously that you might as well not have lived at all—in which case you fail by default.

J. K. ROWLING

Once I started to properly and realistically evaluate my performance, I began to believe in my abilities, and my confidence went up. When I began to trust in my abilities, I was less anxious and had less stress about doing future workshops. Remember, building self-efficacy requires you to shift your beliefs about your abilities. If you are always wearing the pair of glasses with negative and unrealistic lenses, you will not move the bar on your beliefs. Switch out that pair of glasses for a pair that allows you to truly assess how well you are doing and what you need to improve.

Black-and-White Thinking → Allowing Imperfection

You examine your past accomplishment or completed task, and if it was short of perfect or short of the standard you set for yourself, you see it (and possibly yourself) as a failure.

When I was working as the director of education for a national nonprofit, the organization held a successful book launch for the founders. Thanks to an incredibly talented event organizer on our team, hundreds of people showed up and we had national media coverage. We were also successful at securing a local pop singer to sing at the event—and the promoter made it clear that the singer was there to perform, not just provide background music while people chatted and drank. Unfortunately, that is exactly what happened.

The promoter, who was also at the launch, was so angry that she screamed at our event organizer. Our event organizer was devastated. She had worked so hard to create an outstanding event, and now she felt that the night was a horrible bust because this one thing had gone wrong. She could not see the satisfaction of the guests, nor the fantastic press she attracted—she could only see her "colossal" screw-up with the singer. I tried to get her to see otherwise, but she stubbornly held to her belief that the event was a complete failure.

Does this happen to you? If everything does not go perfectly, do you see the total experience as a zero rather than for what it really is? This is perfectionism at its best, but if you want to learn from this experience and raise your efficacy beliefs, you have to let go of perfectionism. Here's why: NOTHING IS EVER PERFECT. If you throw away every performance experience because it was not perfect, you are missing out on very valuable practice, information, and learning. Remember, failures can provide great learning.

As a recovering perfectionist, I know this thinking trap very well. Knowing now that we all have a negativity bias, you know that your brain is working against you in these situations, so it's no surprise that you may fall easily into this trap. And knowing that our brain is hardwired for the negative, we need a rational-brain intervention to help us overcome our overly agitated emotional or limbic brain.

The first step is to have self-awareness. Know when you are focusing on the negative and be aware of how it is affecting you. Know that your limbic brain may be taking over and that you need to "snap out of it." This is not a time to beat yourself up for feeling this way. Here are four questions that can help you see your accomplishment more rationally. These balanced questions are both constructively critical and appreciative.

After a disappointing performance ask yourself:

1. *What went well?* Make a list of everything you think went well. What were all the great results of your hard work? What good came out of it?

2. *How did I contribute to the things that went well?* List all the resources, strengths, and character traits you *personally* contributed to the parts that went well.

3. *What did I learn from this experience that will help me in my next event?* Here you have the opportunity to identify great ways you can do better next time.

By asking these questions, you are proactively turning your focus to things you did right, since your brain is hardwired to only see the bad. You can then still analyze what went wrong, but now with a more balanced view.

Impostor Phenomenon → Taking Ownership of Success

You reject positive experiences or personal successes by insisting that they don't count. People may say, "Wow, that was a great performance!" yet you deny that the results had anything to do with you.

I have a friend who founded an organization to help young people build their confidence and self-esteem. She had instructors at many schools, and she garnered excellent press and attention. She had financial support from top institutions. At her ten-year anniversary, I congratulated her on her amazing accomplishments.

"Oh, it's not me, it's my team," she said modestly. Which I knew was not true, of course—yes, her team was great, but they couldn't have done it without her. I told her that the proper response was "Thank you," which she reluctantly uttered under her breath. Why are we women so reluctant to take credit for our hard work? I think we feel that we want to be inclusive of everyone we work with because, indeed, we don't get places all by ourselves most of the time—but that doesn't mean we cannot take a moment to say, "Dammit, I did a good job." Sometimes all we can see is the tiny drop of water we added to the pond, and we downplay our role in the larger success. We don't take credit for the many ripples that one drop in the pond made. Without that someone who was willing to be that first drop in the pond, nothing begins. Do not underestimate how powerful you are.

When we disqualify the positive, we can fall victim to impostor phenomenon, which, if you recall from chapter 3, perpetuates self-doubt. If we never attribute success to our skills, talent, or knowledge, the next time we attempt the same accomplishment or something similar, we will doubt that we can pull it off. It is only once we can acknowledge that our success was because of our own talent and hard work that we will feel a sense of self-efficacy and peaceful confidence.

A new practice for me is taking the time to reflect on the contributions I made to the success of any endeavor in which I'm involved. Remember, building self-efficacy is about shifting your beliefs about your abilities. If you keep accomplishing without ever believing you are improving, you will never make this important shift in your brain. If you are always giving away your success to others, you will always be perpetuating your feelings of self-doubt.

I find that most people minimize their accomplishments in areas of greatest strength: *It was easy for me, so therefore I must minimize it.* It would be equivalent to Céline Dion downplaying her vocal abilities because they come so naturally to her. Ridiculous! So the next time someone compliments you for an amazing accomplishment, please promise me that you will just say "Thank you" and fully receive it. It is time to own your strengths rather than downplaying them, and to celebrate them.

Being Psychic → Checking for the Truth

You believe that others are thinking badly of you, even though you have no concrete evidence to support this belief.

Years ago, I worked in a building that had a security guard posted in the lobby. She would scowl at me every time I walked by. As I entered the elevator, I would say to my then husband, who worked in the same building and was usually with me, "I swear, she hates me. Every time I pass by, she gives me a dirty look." After several months, I decided to take a new approach. I decided that when I passed her, I would greet her with a pleasant "Hello" and "Have a nice day" or "Have a nice night." The first time I said that, she was so startled, she almost fell off her chair, but she didn't say anything back. I persevered all week. On Friday afternoon as I was leaving, I said, "Have a nice weekend!" This time, she stopped me.

"Wait! Come here."

I was taken aback. I wondered if security guards carried guns. As I approached, she put out her hand to shake mine and said, "Hi, I'm Emily. What's your name?"

"Louisa," I responded, still kind of mystified.

"Louisa, every day you pass by my desk, you say hello and good-bye, and I just want you to know how much I appreciate that. Thank you. No one ever does that."

Wow! Perhaps she wasn't scowling at me after all; maybe she just hated her job. This anecdote illustrates why we need to stop believing in self-created stories: because self-doubt is highly sensitive to social evaluation. What I mean by that is that, as human beings, we are hardwired to care about what other people think. So if you are just making up bad stuff about yourself, without checking for evidence, your negative mind chatter will take away your motivation and your courage to act. If you think someone who is important to you has important criticism about you, ask for that information. If you're not getting along with someone at work and you're conjuring up all sorts of reasons as to why not, invite that person for coffee and see if you can figure out how to move toward a better relationship. You need to check the evidence, because you may find that your mind-reading abilities are not as good as you thought they were.

When I find myself mind reading, I often turn to a good friend or colleague to help me examine things a bit closer. This was the case with another woman who I thought disliked me. When I asked my then husband his opinion of it, he asked me why I thought that. I explained her behavior toward me. He told me that the woman treated everyone in the same way that she treated me, and that, indeed, it was his experience with her as well. That was just the kind of person she was. When I was able to objectively observe her behavior with this new insight,

I found that my husband was right. I was now able to get past how I was feeling about her, based on how I *thought* she was feeling about me, to see her good qualities and open myself up to a better experience with her.

Mike Lipkin, a popular motivational speaker, once said, "If you knew how much time people spent thinking about you, you would not be so concerned with what people thought about you." This stuck with me, and I think of it after every disappointment or setback I experience, and it really helps me bounce back. So remember, most people are absorbed in their own affairs and probably spend very little time thinking about you.

Predicting the Future → Being Open to New Outcomes

Convinced that things will go badly, you believe the outcome is already established. "What's the point of sending my résumé? No one is going to read it anyway," you might say. Or, "What's the point of even asking the guy out? He's just going to say no." By making negative psychic predictions, you self-sabotage your success—and you're just fine with that, because you believe you already know the outcome. You have convinced yourself of it, and this leads to inaction.

At a workshop I delivered for people who had been recently laid off from their jobs, one man said, "Well, I'm in my fifties. No one hires people in their fifties. Employers are looking for younger candidates."

I turned to him and gently asked, "So, this statistic that no one is hiring people in their fifties—is there verified data to support this 'fact,' or did you get that from the little guy sitting on your left shoulder, whispering in your ear?"

He chuckled but stood steadfast. "Well, I have to be realistic—it is harder for people in their fifties to get work." Once again, I asked him where he was getting his data from.

He chuckled again. Silence. Then I reminded him that there were lots of people in our program who were in their fifties who just got jobs the week before—so I had evidence to the contrary. Silence once again. We moved on.

If you truly believe that your negative prediction will in fact be the outcome of your efforts or that that outcome will occur no matter what your efforts are, you will zap yourself of the motivation you require. Remember, beliefs can become self-fulfilling prophecies.

When I catch myself self-sabotaging by predicting a negative future, I listen carefully to what I'm saying and then turn it around by visualizing the opposite. If I'm thinking that no one will respond to my email marketing, I envision many people opening my emails, being excited about what they are reading, and contacting me. If I think my talk will be a flop, I close my eyes and envision many people coming up to me afterward and telling me how helpful it was. If I'm thinking that no men at the bar will find me attractive, I close my eyes before I go and envision many young, hot men approaching me. This simple visualization technique alone can shift your body, change your mood, and boost your confidence. Your demeanor changes and productive behavior follows suit. In chapter 8, I delve deeper into the science behind such visualization.

Catastrophizing → Seeing Opportunities

Irrationally imagining a much worse possible outcome than is realistic.

When I was first forming the CPPA, an unfortunate event took place that I thought would surely jeopardize the whole thing, and I began to catastrophize. I thought there was no way we would be able to move forward with our plans. I had many sleepless nights. Luckily, I had an incredible team who allowed me to see that everything was going to be fine. I decided that if I was going to move forward and create the CPPA, I needed every ounce of positive energy I could muster. So I contemplated all the possible catastrophic scenarios and wrote them down. Then I looked at my list and one by one asked myself, *What is the likelihood this will ever happen?* There were many ridiculous scenarios that I scratched off the list. For those that might actually happen, I planned a strategy for how I would cope. Then I focused my attention on the people we were serving and created an organization that would benefit them most. I stopped wasting my time catastrophizing. I was prepared, just in case something did happen, but my focus was solely on moving forward. What ultimately happened is that none of my catastrophizing scenarios came to be and we proceeded without any barriers.

Often it is not what actually happens to you that can derail you but the stories you make up that can lead you down the rabbit hole. We can take mundane events and turn them into huge obstacles that we then ruminate about. You must master your self-talk if you want to persevere to the finish line. Mastering your self-talk is critical to improving your performance, building your confidence, and finding the courage to act. Here is an exercise founded in cognitive behavioral therapy that can help you master your inner dialogue.

EXERCISE: **SEPARATING FACTS FROM STORIES**

This exercise involves two steps: separating the facts from the story you tell yourself, and disputing the story. I've created a fictitious scenario to illustrate how this exercise works.

Step 1: Separating Facts from Stories

Let's say you are at an important business event and you have an opportunity to speak to someone who is a big name in your industry. You would like to make a good first impression. As you chat you blurt out something that is really (and I mean really) stupid. The person chuckles and the conversation moves on. What is the first thing that comes to your head? I can take a guess: *What an idiot! I had the guy in the palm of my hand, and now he must think I am a complete bimbo! He'll never take a call from me now.* This is an example of automatic negative thoughts, or ANTs. Using this scenario, let's separate out the facts from the stories:

What Are the Facts?	What Stories Are You Telling Yourself about This Situation? (ANTS)	What Is the Evidence for the Story?
I said something I believed was really stupid, to someone really important.	I am an idiot!	Just because I said something that was less than stellar doesn't mean I am an idiot. I have lots of evidence to the contrary.
	I had the guy in the palm of my hand, and now he must think I am a complete bimbo!	I don't know if he thinks I am a complete bimbo. I didn't ask him.
	He'll never take a call from me now.	I have no idea if he will take my call in the future or not. I have no evidence either way.

Step 2: Disputing the Stories

Once you have separated the facts from the stories you are telling yourself, the next step is to dispute those stories. Cognitive behavioral therapists use the technique of disputation to get us to challenge our negative ways of talking to ourselves. Essentially, disputation is about challenging the story in your head. The first step in disputation is to have awareness of what you are saying.

For one week, write down the ANTs that arise when you face an adversity. Become aware of what you are saying in your head (or out loud) after a setback. By becoming aware, you can begin to see how hard you are being on yourself. I bet you would never talk to a friend like this, and yet somehow you feel perfectly comfortable talking to yourself so poorly.

When the week is over, take a good look at your list. The more you can understand how and when you are engaging in negative self-talk, the easier it will be for you to dispute or challenge it. In the following week, write down what you say to yourself after being confronted by adversity, and begin to challenge those thoughts. Know that ANTs are not just thoughts but beliefs that limit your self-efficacy. Continuing with the example above, here is what disputation sounds like:

ANT: *I am an idiot!*
Disputation: *You are an intelligent person, with two university degrees. You're not an idiot.*

ANT: *Now he must think I am a complete bimbo.*
Disputation: *You are trying to mind read. You have no idea what he thinks of you.*

ANT: *He'll never take a call from me now.*
Disputation: *I don't know that. He didn't say that. He seemed to like me, and he will probably answer if I call.*

What you will find is that, over time, as you dispute all the negative stories you are making up, your ANTs will begin to disappear. After many years of practice, I no longer have ANTs. You have had these ANTs for many years, maybe even your whole life, so the technique of disputing ANTs can take some time to master. Do not be discouraged if it takes you months or even years to change your self-talk. Keep practicing every day until you have. I promise you, it will be the best thing you will ever do for yourself.

Confidence Habits

- Master your self-talk after disappointments and successes to increase your self-efficacy, fuel your next step, and maximize learning.
- Master the techniques of getting yourself out of common thinking traps:
    a. Catch yourself when using the negative lens, and try to be more realistic.
    b. Recognize that being imperfect doesn't mean you did a bad job.
    c. Take ownership for your success and stop feeling like an impostor.
    d. Stop guessing what other people think. You're not psychic!
    e. Envision the outcome you want when predicting the future.
    f. Stop catastrophizing and just get the work done.
- Master the art of disputing automatic negative thoughts.

7

How to Embrace Failure

NOW WE HAVE some constructive things we can say to ourselves after a disappointment. But how do we bounce back from an epic fail? If you truly want to take yourself to the next level, embracing failure will be an important skill to have.

I laugh when people say "Make failure your friend" or "Learn to love failure." I think these people must be high on ecstasy. Who loves failure? I'm writing this book on self-confidence, and I still don't like it when I fail. And I'm not alone. Fear of failure is always the number one reason given when I ask people why they are not going after their dreams.

So what is it about failure that makes people go to such great lengths to avoid it? As I mention in chapter 3, research shows it is not so much about the failure itself but about how it feels when we fail in front of others. If I were on a desert island

and no one was watching me try something and fail a hundred times, I'm sure I would attempt many more things than I would otherwise. Researchers have shed light on how situations become significantly more stressful for us when we know we are being watched and evaluated. There seems to be a preoccupation with what other people think. It's as if we believe everyone is watching our every move for some reason.

Two researchers at the University of California, Irvine, Sally Dickerson and Margaret Kemeny, conducted a meta-analysis of 208 studies on stress.[34] They wanted to know what kind of events triggered the highest peaks in cortisol. Cortisol is the stress hormone our body releases when we feel under threat. What Dickerson and Kemeny found is that the highest peaks in cortisol occur when tasks include some social-evaluative threat, where others could negatively judge our performance, and particularly when the outcome of the performance is uncontrollable. When we embark on something new, the outcomes are usually unknown to us and thus uncontrollable.

All this may just be the perfect storm that could very well be stopping us from trying anything new. All those feelings of shame that come flooding in when we even think about failing—it's uncomfortable. But changing our feelings about failure is like trying to persuade someone to walk into a small cage with a wild lion. The emotional part of our brain goes on high alert when we think we could publicly fail, which means our brain is one more obstacle in this battle to embrace failure. Knowing this, here are two ways to help you embrace failure and manage it more effectively.

Do Not Make Your Self-Worth Contingent on Success or Failure

In chapter 4, I talked about the work of Dr. Jennifer Crocker on contingent self-esteem. If you judge yourself after every achievement, your feelings of self-esteem will go up with each success and down with each disappointment.

I used to work with women who had been out of the workforce and on social assistance for many years. I learned that many of them were in those circumstances because they were having trouble overcoming problems in their lives. Some had been beaten as children, some had experienced sexual abuse, some were fleeing domestic violence. Regardless of the reasons, they all suffered from low self-esteem. On a particularly difficult day, when they all seemed to be pushing back on everything I said, I stopped the class and pulled out a crisp twenty-dollar bill from my wallet. I asked for a volunteer to join me at the front of the class.

"What is this?" I asked her, waving the bill in my hand.

"A twenty-dollar bill," she responded.

"How much is it worth in Canada?" I asked.

"Twenty dollars." She was wondering where I was going with all this.

"And if you go to any store in Canada and want to buy something for twenty dollars or less, can you use this to pay?"

"Of course."

"Good," I said. Then I gave her the twenty-dollar bill and asked her to crumple it up. She looked at me kind of funny, but she took it and crumpled it up. Then I asked her to throw it on the ground and stomp on it. She did. I asked her to stomp heavily on it, with both feet. Now she really got into it, stomping, kicking, and smushing it. The whole class was cheering her on at this point. When she was done, I picked up and unraveled the crumpled, dirty paper. I tried to flatten it a bit. It barely resembled the crisp, new bill I had pulled out of my wallet.

I asked the woman, "How much is it worth now?"

Her eyes widened. "Twenty dollars."

You could have heard a pin drop. Tears welled in the women's eyes as they all came to the realization that just because life had stomped on them, crushed them, and left them crumpled, it did not mean they did not have value. The *same* value as before. Just because they had made mistakes and chosen the wrong strategies at times did not mean they were worthless. The same goes for you.

A healthy way to reflect on failures is to be curious about them. "I am curious how this could have failed so miserably." Judging yourself is only going to spiral you down; instead, focus on the strategies, resources, preparation, conditions, and circumstances that led to the failure. Maybe you didn't work hard enough? Maybe it was the wrong strategy? Who could give you some positive constructive feedback? Stay curious about your failure and think about what you would do differently next time.

I had a workshop participant who was a young and talented stand-up comedian. She believed that the best way to improve her skills as a comedian was to book as many gigs as possible. After all, the only way you get better at comedy is by practicing in front of a live audience. This practice would allow her to improve and reach higher levels of success. But she really wasn't comfortable booking gigs because she didn't feel she was good enough yet. It was uncomfortable standing up there while no one laughed at her jokes or, worse, booed her off the stage. So she was avoiding booking the gigs. After learning about the science of self-confidence in my workshop, she booked as many comedy gigs as she could. Instead of focusing on how she *felt* after each performance (her self-esteem), she focused on what worked and what didn't work (that specific performance). Recently, I learned that she created a one-woman show that premiered at an indie theater festival. Not making your self-esteem contingent on your accomplishments can be a powerful thing.

After a failure, contingent self-esteem says: *What is wrong with me?*

After a failure, noncontingent self-esteem says: *What was wrong with that particular performance/approach/strategy?*

Can you feel the difference?

Let's try this. Imagine you have just cooked a meal for your in-laws. You can tell they didn't enjoy it because they left half of it on their plates. In fact, you yourself didn't think it was that tasty. If your self-esteem was contingent on making this a good meal, you would be saying things to yourself like *I'm such a loser. They are going to think I'm such a horrible daughter-in-law if I can't even cook a meal for my husband. I am failing as a wife.* When your self-esteem is not contingent on making this a good meal, you would instead be saying things like *Well, that was disappointing. Trying to cook from a new recipe when the in-laws are over was probably not a good idea. Next time, cook something I've had success with in the past.* In the first scenario, you are criticizing yourself as a person; in the second scenario, you are criticizing your approach to preparing the meal. Decide that regardless of the outcome, you will always feel good about yourself. I promise that if you can begin to make this shift of focus after every disappointment, you will make huge strides in embracing failure.

Practice Self-Compassion

According to Dr. Kristin Neff, a leading researcher on self-compassion, several studies support the idea that people who are more self-compassionate have greater perceived self-confidence. "First of all," says Dr. Neff, "when we criticize ourselves constantly, when we cut ourselves down, we are pulling the rug out from underneath ourselves. We are giving ourselves the message, sometimes constantly, that we are not good enough, we are a failure and that impacts our beliefs and our ability to do well."[35] Many people are so hard on themselves because they feel it is the only way to motivate themselves, but the research on self-compassion shows that the opposite is true. Being highly self-compassionate can actually help you perform better.[36]

Another detrimental consequence of regularly berating yourself after a failure is that you will stop trying because the risk is too high. But if you treat yourself kindly and with compassion after failure, you become less afraid of failure. When you know you will find a compassionate friend after failure—yourself—it's almost as if you create your own cushion for that fall.

We ask ourselves, "Who am I to be brilliant, gorgeous, talented, fabulous?" Actually, who are you not to be?

MARIANNE WILLIAMSON

We know that failure is our best teacher. "When it's safe to fail, it's safe to try," says Dr. Neff. We know from Dr. Bandura's work (discussed in chapter 4) that trying things out, learning from our experiences, and trying again is our most effective way to improve self-efficacy. Self-compassion, then, can fuel our motivation to try. When you practice this technique regularly, you begin to trust in yourself. You begin to trust that you will always have a kind friend who will comfort you and be kind to you.

Self-compassion not only helps with self-confidence but has been shown to reduce self-criticism, depression, anxiety, and rumination, and to improve well-being. Self-compassion is also positively related to self-esteem, meaning it can help us feel better about ourselves too.

The research is clear: self-compassionate people are much more likely to keep trying, so it is very beneficial for both confidence and motivation. I asked Dr. Neff if she would share the three elements of self-compassion we should all be practicing when going through a rough time or trying to recover from an epic failure.[37]

1. Become Aware of Your Own Suffering

Recognize that what you are going through is tough. Don't suppress your feelings, but allow yourself to feel the feelings you are experiencing at that moment.

Often we suppress our feelings, thinking that we have to be happy all the time, wondering what is wrong with us when we are not happy. In today's society, we have such pressure to appear to be happy all the time that when we are not feeling happy, we have one more reason to beat up on ourselves. When we allow ourselves to feel the full range of feelings that happen as a result of life circumstances, without beating ourselves up for them, we can release what we need to release and then get back on track. So if you have just suffered a colossal failure, it's okay to be embarrassed about it! It is much healthier to feel your full range of emotions without suppression. You just don't want to stay stuck there. Feel the feelings and then move on by engaging in some of the self-talk techniques I describe in chapter 6.

One word of caution here: if you are feeling extremely overwhelmed by your feelings and cannot cope with your regular routine, don't be afraid to seek professional help. I am quite happy and have many psychological resources to help me deal with whatever life brings me, but when I'm going through a period of extremely high stress, I do visit my therapist, who is a licensed psychologist, who offers me professional support. This is one way I continue to manage my psychological well-being. When Olympians are preparing for the Olympics, even when they are at the top of their game, they hire more coaches, not fewer. That is because being in the Olympics is hard. When you are going through the roughest times of your life—your "life Olympics"—recognize that you may need professionals to help you through it. Getting professional help may be the single most important thing you do for yourself, your family, and your self-confidence.

2. Be Kind to Yourself

Treat yourself as your best friend would treat you. When you catch yourself beating yourself up, ask yourself, *Is this what my best friend would say right now?* Replace your words of defeat with kind words your best friend would say.

One day I had an aha moment *while* I was being particularly harsh with myself. I had a moment of clarity when I actually heard what I was saying to myself. The words were absolutely awful. And I realized that if my spouse, best friend, coworker, or even a stranger spoke to me that way, I would kick them to the curb. I would think they were being abusive, and I wouldn't stand for it. So why did I stand for it coming from myself? Who the hell did I think I was? That day was a game-changer for me. I chose to trade in that terrible internal friend for one who truly loves me. Now I am followed around all day by a truly loving and compassionate friend (me!), who says kind and encouraging things even after a disappointment, just like my best friend would. Who will you choose to have following you around all day? Your worst enemy or your most compassionate friend? Remember, you get to choose, so choose wisely.

A helpful technique that can help you bounce back from failure, especially in the moment, is to create a mantra for yourself. One of my favorite self-compassionate mantras, which I say after a failure or disappointment, is *Louisa, you are doing your best.* (A variation is *Louisa, you did your best with what you had.*) When I am feeling the sting of a failure, I say this mantra. I have it ready, top of mind, to invoke when I need to. I love my mantra because I tend to be hardest on myself when many people witnessed me failing at something. After I say it, I feel so much better about everything. I can just feel my emotions calm.

Find a mantra that works for you. I often ask people in my workshops what their self-compassionate mantra is and they say things like "Tomorrow is another day" or "Everything is a learning experience." Take a moment now and think of your own self-compassion mantra. Find one that works for you. Tweet me at @louisajewell and let me know your self-compassionate mantra.

3. Understand That You Are Not Alone

Understand that what you are going through is part of the common human experience. Whatever failure you experience is really no different from how millions of others have failed before you. Once we accept that we are not perfect and have flaws, just like everyone else on the planet, we stop asking "What's wrong with me?" and instead say, "Oh, I'm just like a million other people." Focus on your good qualities and celebrate them instead.

I'll never forget the day my husband of nineteen years came to me and said that he was not happy. He had decided he was moving out. Now, you need to understand that this man is the love of my life, my soulmate. I always thought we would grow old together. He is such a wonderful man. We love each other deeply, we respect and support each other, we encourage each other when life is challenging, we don't fight, and we enjoy each other's company. I was deeply in love with him. I adored him. So you can imagine how shocked and devastated I was with the news that he was leaving. I mean, I knew our marriage wasn't perfect, but I was not expecting it to end over the troubles we had.

It would have been easy for me to beat myself up in this moment and ask how I could have been so clueless, so out of touch with his reality, but I did not go there. The reason I did not go down the rabbit hole (even for five minutes) is that I have been practicing self-compassion for more than ten years, so when this happened, self-compassion became one of my default ways of being during the worst time of my life. I always say, "You can't start practicing for the Olympics when you get to the Olympics." What I mean is that being self-compassionate during a crisis may be more difficult than during noncrisis times because you are already emotionally depleted and it may be more difficult to control your thoughts. But when you have been practicing self-compassion for many years and it has become a habitual way of handling and bouncing back from a failure or crisis, it comes naturally.

When my husband left me, I practiced Dr. Neff's three elements of self-compassion. I gave myself permission to grieve and sit in my profound sadness. I loved running through a local forest near my house every day, and sometimes I would stop and sit by the stream and just sob and sob. I went to hot yoga every day and cried for the hour. Luckily for me, everyone is sweating so much in hot yoga that no one notices the difference between crying and perspiring! I treated myself like my best friends would treat me. I said kind words to myself. I stayed away from judgmental people and spoke only to my best girlfriends, who I knew would be supportive and say kind things. I ate better, I exercised more, I booked massages, and I dressed nicely every day. I recognized that this has happened to millions of nice, loving, intelligent women, so oddly enough, I never once asked what was wrong to me. I am not perfect, just as no one else is. Self-compassion saved me.

Self-compassion is different from self-pity. Self-pity is when you are so absorbed in your own problems that you forget there are many others experiencing something similar or worse, and as a result you amplify your own suffering. And when you become so self-absorbed, it is difficult for you to get out of your own personal suffering. Some of you might be wondering, if I, Louisa, am always kind to myself, how am I ever going to learn from my mistakes and become a better person or better at what I want to get better at? Well, I engaged in constructive questioning, as described in chapter 6. Instead of beating myself up, I asked myself, *What was my contribution to this separation? What could I have done differently to have prevented this? How can I be a better partner the next time around?* All these questions allowed me to explore how I can improve for next time without feeling bad about myself. As a result, I am emerging a stronger, wiser woman.

I still find there are days when I cannot breathe because I am overwhelmed with sadness, but treating myself with kindness has had the greatest positive impact on my well-being and my productivity. In fact, in the year following my separation, I doubled my revenues and had more business than I have ever had. Going through the divorce process is a profoundly sad experience that will have a tremendous effect on my life, but I refuse to let it affect my confidence or lower my self-esteem. Practicing self-compassion has allowed me to be compassionate toward my ex-husband as well. We are actually having a very positive divorce; in fact, some people comment that our divorce is more positive than their marriages. (Maybe that is the topic of my next book!)

Here is an exercise that will help you move on from failure. Let's face it. Nobody likes to fail. But the more you wallow in your self-pity, the less time and energy you have to go after your dreams. Feelings of failure can decrease self-efficacy or be your best opportunity to learn. Not all failure is the same, and it can be a lot harder to bounce back after a major setback. Some people ask me, "Louisa, what if the most likely scenario *is* the worst-case scenario?" For example, what if your business *is* going to go bankrupt or you epically failed on an important project or the love of your life just walked out on you? Then I use this technique to remind myself that I am resilient and I have what it takes to bounce back and recover from setbacks. The more you can learn about your own resilience strengths, the more resources you will have on hand to get yourself back on track after a setback.

EXERCISE: **KNOW YOUR RESILIENCE STRENGTHS**

Think of a time in your life when something important to you did not turn out as you had hoped—a time of adversity and yet you managed to persevere and successfully overcame the challenge. It could have been a failed project, a failed relationship, or maybe an unexpected illness. The best stories are stories of adversity that you successfully managed. Write about this experience in your notebook. To get started, consider these questions:

1. What did you do to cope with the situation? What did you do to cope with your feelings? Write down all of your best coping strategies that got you through.
2. Reflect on *everything* you did to successfully navigate your way through this challenge. Did you read books? Did you persevere? Did you show empathy? Did you use your social intelligence? Were you forgiving? Did you adopt an attitude of gratitude? For example, when my good friend was faced with a breast cancer diagnosis, she read a ton of books and attended seminars on nutrition. Her strength of "love of learning" really kicked in at that time. In fact, she was so obsessed about learning as much as she could that she actually became a holistic nutritionist. I'm happy to report that she is in good health, several years later. When I suffer a disappointment, I tend to focus on what I am grateful for. I use

my strength of gratitude to get me through. Reflect on what you did to get you through and see if you can identify your own resilience strengths. Knowing what works for you at your time of need can be very helpful information for the future.

3 Did anything in your life change for the better as a result of the adversity? As I've mentioned, I fell into a deep depression after my fourth miscarriage. Even though I would never wish this for me again or for anyone else, my depression sent me on a quest to understand how to stay psychologically healthy. That depression brought me to my current life path. Had that depression not happened, I may have never gone on a quest to learn more about psychological well-being. But because I did, I teach positive psychology to thousands of people every year and I absolutely love it. I meet the most incredible people, I learn about fascinating topics, and I feel honored to be improving the lives of so many people. My miscarriages were unwanted, and yet I can see now that all experiences in my life are valuable. Acceptance is a powerful tool for energy management that fuels our motivation to keep pursuing our dreams. The more I can be open to learning from it and accepting of it, the easier it will be to move on without getting stuck.

What did you learn about yourself from this exercise? Hopefully you have identified the strategies, strengths, and resources you use to get yourself through adversities in your life. Keep these top of mind, to remind yourself that you are stronger than you think. Remind yourself that every failure, no matter how disappointing, can lead to positive outcomes. This will make you more hopeful as you navigate your way through future adversities.

Confidence Habits

- Recognize that failure can provide some of the best learning experiences.
- Do not allow your self-esteem to be contingent on either your successes or failures.
- Begin practicing self-compassion right away—before you experience a crisis or failure.
- Identify your resilience strengths and keep them top of mind, to get you through future adversities in your life.

8

Seeing to Believe

RESEARCH SHOWS THAT we gain confidence by seeing others succeeding, as that shifts our brain into believing we can be successful too. Even *imagining* ourselves being successful can shift our beliefs about our own capabilities and reduce self-doubt and boost confidence. In this chapter, we explore the influence that role models and visualization have on us.

Find Role Models

We tend to see others, especially those who are more like us, as an effective barometer of our own capabilities. If I have a friend who is similar to me in age, gender, socioeconomic status, and education, and she is successful at something I am striving for, this could be a powerful source of self-efficacy for me. Research shows that age and gender similarities have the greatest effects on efficacy beliefs. That is to say, the best role models to boost self-efficacy are those similar in age and gender to you.

For years, I was ten pounds heavier than I wanted to be. I had resigned myself to the "fact" that I was always going to be that weight, and I didn't believe that I could shift my "new normal" to being ten pounds lighter. Then one day I ran into my friend Sabrina. Sabrina has this incredibly rockin' body. It got me thinking, if Sabrina, who is my age, can have a body like that, why can't I? It was actually the first time I thought about my weight in a new way. Seeing Sabrina shifted my beliefs about myself. So I asked Sabrina how she got her gorgeous body, and she told me she did one hour of hot yoga every day and ate a vegan diet. I thought, *I can do that!*

So I found a studio that offers hot yoga classes and began to go every day. I would look at my schedule for the day and then look at the yoga studio's schedule, and I'd decide which class fit best. I didn't become a vegan, but I decided to eat a more vegetarian-like diet, cutting meat from most of my meals. The pounds started to come off! I was thrilled. Over a few months' time, I lost twelve pounds. Unfortunately, all the weight came off my butt, just when big butts were back in style, but I was still happy with the results!

Seeing a role model similar to us be successful can also backfire, though. When we are feeling insecure about ourselves and we see a friend just like us achieve success, we may judge ourselves negatively. Some people spend a lot of time absorbed in social media, constantly comparing themselves with others who are farther along the success scale and making themselves miserable! For years, I was jealous of a certain colleague's successes. I would think, *I am just like her—how come she's seeing all that success and I'm not?* This actually made me feel bad about myself and did not motivate me to succeed. I tended to avoid interacting with her because she threatened my self-esteem. It was nothing she ever did to me; it was totally in my mind.

Once I learned about how role models can have a positive effect, I started to see how I could learn and be inspired by this colleague, rather than shy away from her. I reached out to her to ask her how she became successful. She was amazingly helpful and generous, sharing a great deal of information with me. Then she began to help me in so many other ways too. Every time there is a way I can help her, I do my best to. She has become a fantastic source of inspiration and motivation. I learn from her every day, and as a result, my business is flourishing.

Focusing on your role models' instructional value instead of comparing yourself against them is the best way to leverage your role models for the most effective efficacy building. In other words, ask, "What can I learn from this role model?" rather than seeing them as a threat. Believe in abundance—that there is enough success for all of us.

One of my favorite sayings is from Deborah Poneman and Marci Shimoff, a dynamic duo who run the year-long program "Your Year of Miracles." I participated in the program three years in a row. They recommend that when you find yourself jealous of someone else's wealth, success, or talent, say to yourself, *And some of that for me, please!* Jealousy puts you in a state of negative emotion, which does not fuel motivation. Inspiration, by contrast, puts you in a state of positive emotion, which motivates.

Choose Role Models Who Are at a Similar Level of Mastery or Slightly Higher

The level of mastery a role model is at will affect self-efficacy beliefs. If I see someone who has been doing a certain task for twenty years and I am just starting with it, it will be harder for me to believe I can do it too. People who are similar to us or slightly higher in ability provide the most information about whether I can succeed as well.

One exception to this is if I discover they started off in a situation similar to mine. For example, I discovered Marie Forleo many years ago and began to follow her. She is an expert in online marketing and has her own Web TV show.[38] I wanted to create video blogs, but when I saw her blogs, it was obvious to me that they were professionally produced. I figured it must cost a fortune and that I could never create videos of high enough quality, so I was discouraged to start. Then one day I watched one of her videos in which she traces the history of her video blog. She shows her first blogs from years ago. They were not professionally produced or scripted, but they still had an important message to share. She showed me that you can start with humble beginnings, which convinced me that I could get better over time, just like she had. So I started my video blogs—which are not perfect, but it's a start! They've brought greater attention to my work and company, and my business has begun to grow and grow. I've learned that even when one's performance is not perfectly crafted, people may still be interested.

Coping Role Models

We may also seek out role models for their coping capabilities. Sometimes we have a great idea but it gets shut down time after time, and after a while we give up on it entirely. Thinking of how the creators of the Chicken Soup for the Soul series persevered, even after 144 rejections, inspires me. Seth Godin, considered one of the best marketers in the world, once said, "People don't reject you, they reject your story." It's not that the Chicken Soup creators had a bad idea; it's just that publishers were not recognizing the value of the books. Now when I get rejected, I think that my message or my marketing is not right, and I try again. Keep that in mind the next time you face rejection.

Seeing others struggle and ultimately succeed boosts our self-efficacy in many ways. First, seeing people struggle before succeeding reminds us of our own struggles, and that struggle is probably a necessary part of success. When we are struggling, we often think something must be wrong with us without realizing that every worthwhile endeavor comes with some sort of learning curve. Second, watching someone persevere after a setback keeps our spirits up by teaching us that perseverance eventually brings success. We learn that perseverance, not just talent, is important to success. Research has found that it is not the most talented people who succeed; it is the people who persevere over the long term. Finally, we learn what successful people say to themselves while they are struggling, which encourages us to engage in our own positive self-talk.

If you do not have a role model for what you would like to do, I encourage you to seek one. Find role models who are most like you, and ask if you can interview them or take them for coffee. Here are some questions to ask:

- How did you begin to do what you do?
- What did you do to be successful in that role?
- What suggestions do you have that would help someone like me get started?
- What advice do you have for me?

Also remember to ask them coping questions like:

- What was your biggest obstacle and how did you overcome it?
- When things didn't go your way, what would you say to yourself to keep on track?
- What did you do to boost your confidence when you suffered a disappointing failure?

Most people shy away from approaching others and asking these kinds of questions because they think, *Why would they spend time with a potential competitor?* or *Why would they take the time for me?* But the fact of the matter is that most successful people are more than happy to help others who are just getting started.

When Kathy Korman Frey went to Harvard University to study business, she soon discovered that every case study about entrepreneurs featured only male entrepreneurs. Knowing the importance of having female role models, Korman Frey created an online case study database called the Hot Mommas Project (www.hotmommasproject.org). In the collection of stories, women share their insights on how they successfully balance work and life. Some are stories of corporate success, while others are stories about everyday challenges. Reading the stories can boost self-efficacy, as you see yourself in them.

Korman Frey has spoken to thousands of women about self-confidence and believes that, in comparison, self-efficacy is a more action-oriented type of confidence that drives women as entrepreneurs. When I asked her about women's experience with self-doubt, she said it was relentless, universal, and defied boundaries. It didn't matter whom she was talking to—whether a woman fresh out of college or a highly established surgeon—self-doubt plagued them all. If we want to be at the table, we need to deal with self-doubt.

Korman Frey does not recommend having just one mentor in your life; she recommends five at least. In her research she found that women who had five or more mentors showed a 20 percent increase in their perception of self-confidence when compared with those who had fewer than five. Role models not only act as a source of support and encouragement and proof that "it can be done"; they also offer instructional value on how to successfully navigate any new endeavor.

Mastermind Groups

One of the most effective strategies I have employed to surround myself with role models who are learning to cope just like me is participating in mastermind groups. Mastermind groups were made popular by Jack Canfield through his book *The Success Principles*.[39] A mastermind group is a group of four to six people who work together to actively support each other in working toward their personal goals. I find groups of four to be the perfect size, as it gives everyone time for maximum sharing. I belong to two mastermind groups, each for different goals in my life.

We get together for two hours once a month over video conference, and we share wins, goals, resources, encouragement, and expertise. Each of us has thirty minutes "on the floor." We usually begin our thirty minutes with a five-minute update about special wins or setbacks. In the next five minutes, we describe a question, issue, problem, or opportunity that we want feedback and guidance on. A timekeeper keeps us on track, so that everyone gets their full thirty minutes. In between meetings, we are always there for each other, supporting and encouraging one another.

For example, when one of my groups met, I was in the process of formulating a new talk for corporations, and I wanted advice on topics that I could talk about that would appeal to a corporate market. The group members came up with many approaches on how I could figure out what corporations want to hear about and what's important to them, and they shared their experiences of talking to corporations. Then we brainstormed ideas. I walked away from that meeting with a million ideas, and I formulated two new talks to market to new clients. That is just one example of the valuable exchange I have with my mastermind group.

You will want your mastermind group to consist of people who are already where you'd like to be in your life, or who are at least a level above you in certain areas of interest to you. For example, you may choose people who are more established speakers or authors (if that is where you want to stretch and grow), and they may choose you for your marketing abilities (where they want to stretch and grow). Everyone in the group has something to offer. One of my mastermind groups focuses on business goals and attainments, while my other group focuses on maintaining positive mental energy. Both help me achieve my professional and personal goals. The people in these groups act as role models for me. I see how they succeed and what they continue to do to succeed, and it inspires me to do the same. They are a continual source of self-efficacy.

Mental Rehearsal (aka Visualization)

Just by sitting quietly with your eyes closed and imagining a successful run-through of your intended performance you can have a positive impact on your self-efficacy. These boosts are not as powerful as the ones you might experience after a real successful performance experience, but they are a boost nevertheless. Sports psychologists have known this for decades and have used mental rehearsal to train Olympic athletes, international champions, and top professional athletes.

In one meta-analysis of thirty-six studies testing the effects of visualization on *performance*—with 3,214 participants in total—the researchers found that mental practice is an effective way to enhance performance for both cognitive and physical tasks.[40] They found positive results even with people who had never performed the task, which indicated that this is a performance-enhancing strategy for newbies too. The data support the claim that mental practice is not as effective as actually practicing the task but still has a positive effect. Visualization cannot be seen as a replacement for actually doing the work but, rather, complements your endeavors and goals.

The research also found that the positive effects of mental practice on performance, not surprisingly, decline over time. The greatest effects were found just before performing the task; after two weeks, the benefits declined to one-half their original strength. After three weeks, the effects had almost disappeared. If you are going to use visualization to boost your self-efficacy, it might be best to engage in it on a regular basis, perhaps every morning or at least once every week.

Many researchers have found that visualizing for long periods may have a weaker effect than if visualizing for short periods. They believe that longer durations may lead to a loss of concentration and that shorter durations—less than twenty minutes each—are optimal. I visualize my goals for five minutes every morning. This keeps them top of mind, and it also energizes me for the day.

Process vs. Outcome Visualization

The kind of visualizing you do makes a difference. Shelley Taylor, Lien Pham, and colleagues at the University of California, Los Angeles, conducted a study to see if visualizing the *process* toward a successful outcome had effects different from those if you were to just visualize the *outcome*.[41] They had 101

Whatever you
can do, or dream
you can, begin
it. Boldness has
genius, power,
and magic in it.

GOETHE

students, for five minutes every day for one week, visualize getting an A on their upcoming exams. One group visualized just the *process*—what it would take to get an A (studying hard); the other group visualized getting an A. What they found was that the group that visualized only the outcome received an average of 72 percent on the exam, 2 percent lower than the class average, whereas the group that visualized the process achieved an average score of 81 percent, which represented a score that was 6.6 percent higher than the class average.

Not only did the outcome group do worse on the exam, but they studied less and were less motivated. Researchers conclude that visualizing only a positive outcome may be convincing our brain that the goal has already been achieved and therefore nothing more is required. Visualizing the process instead puts us in a state of readiness to act, and we move into action much more easily, which also reduces procrastination. If your brain thinks you have initiated the process of making something happen, you are more likely to begin in real life. If you are procrastinating or having a particularly unproductive day, take some time to visualize yourself going through the process of successfully getting the task done. I find this can kick-start me on days when I am feeling stuck.

Reduce Stress for the Task

I use mental rehearsal to help me calm my nerves before a big event or important meeting. If I have a meeting scheduled with the CEO of a big company to sell my services, I close my eyes and quietly spend five minutes envisioning a successful meeting. I see myself speaking with ease and the CEO fully engaged in what I am saying. I imagine the CEO saying things like "Wow, Louisa, your work sounds so fascinating. We'd love to have you do some work for us." And "You have come to us exactly at the right time. This is just what we need right now." When I envision a successful meeting, I completely relax. When I'm in the meeting I have more confidence, which in turn makes people feel more confident about me. Haven't you found that when people are not confident in themselves, you question their abilities? I visualize success before every big talk, conference, and workshop. Try this before your next big event and see how it can help you shift into confidence.

Vision Boards

Vision boards have become quite popular in the past decade, especially since the release of the movie and book *The Secret*. A vision board is a collection of pictures cut out of magazines or drawn images that represent goals you want to achieve, assembled on a poster board, and on which you can focus attention every day. Spending a few minutes every day visualizing your goals keeps them top of mind. As you go about your day, you are now looking for opportunities that allow you to fulfill your goals. Vision boards that include pictures of you or others engaging in activities around the *process* of getting to your ultimate goal are more effective than just outcome visuals.

Primers

Vision boards can also act as powerful primers. The goal-setting literature confirms that consciously setting goals typically improves performance. What most people don't know is that planting a goal in your subconscious is an effective way to improve performance. It can be as simple as just posting a picture of your achieved goal in plain sight or exposing yourself to certain words.

When my daughter was applying to a prestigious high school, we visited the school and I took pictures of her walking the halls and pretending to open her locker, as if she were already a student there. We printed those pictures and put them up around the house so she could see them every day while she studied for her entrance exams and prepared for her interview. A few months later, she was accepted at the school.

Research shows that a primed goal has greater motivational effects on performance than a nonprimed goal.[42] In one study, employees at a call center solicited funds for a university. The control group was given a financial goal to achieve and presented with printed instructions on how to solicit donations. The experimental group was also given a goal and received the exact same package of instructions with one difference: the instructions were printed over a color photograph of a woman winning a race. What the researchers found was that employees who were primed with a goal for achievement via the photo of the woman winning a race raised significantly more money from donors than did their colleagues in the control group.

That picture of success subconsciously boosted self-efficacy.

My friend Caroline Adams Miller suggests to prime your subconscious by making your password a phrase that will motivate you toward your goal. For example, if you are trying to quit smoking, your password might be "healthy lungs." Every time you type your password, you are priming your memory to think of your healthy lungs, which then may improve your willpower not to smoke.

Self-Modeling

In a fascinating research study, Dr. Daniel Kirschenbaum at the University of Wisconsin asked a group of bowlers to review their performance after each bowling session.[43] He divided the bowlers into two groups. Those in group one reviewed only what they did well and were asked to remind themselves to repeat more of the good bowling techniques. Those in group two were asked to review their performance and indicate what they had done poorly and remind themselves to avoid making the same mistakes in the following rounds.

Which group of bowlers do you think improved their bowling performance? The bowlers who focused on what they did well showed as much as 100 percent improvement in bowling scores when compared with the other group! Self-modeling is often more successful with self-doubters than instructional modeling, because when we spend time reflecting on our past successful performance, we strongly believe we can do it again; we know these successes are authentic rather than contrived.

By performing the task and reflecting on what went well, then performing the task again, we are focused on progressive mastery. We have clear information on how to best perform the skill, and we strengthen our belief in our capabilities at the same time. Also, we feel positive emotions when we reflect on a success, which fuels us to try harder in the next round.

Learning from others and visualizing are two important sources of self-efficacy that can boost your confidence and give you the courage to act. Think about how you can adopt these habits as a daily practice to keep you confident no matter what is happening in your life. Here is a powerful visualizing technique; I find it especially useful when feeling particularly hopeless.

EXERCISE: **THE MIRACLE QUESTIONS**

One of my favorite series of questions in solution-focused coaching are the miracle questions, devised by Insoo Kim Berg, pioneer of solution-focused brief therapy, and which go something like this:

Suppose tonight while you sleep a miracle happens... the miracle being that your dreams and/or goals have all been achieved, just like that. But you do not know about the miracle since you were asleep. Close your eyes and really visualize what your life is like after this miracle has happened.

- How, the next morning, will you discover that this miracle must have occurred?

- What is happening now that was not happening before the miracle occurred? (List as many things as you can think of.)
- What will be different? (List as many things as you can think of.)
- How will you react differently? How will you *be* different?
- Who might notice that this miracle has happened to you? (List everyone who would notice.)
- How will they notice?
- What else might they notice is different about you?

If you are feeling that your confidence will never increase around something you really want to pursue, or you think that you will never achieve your goals, these questions can very quickly shift your brain and your body toward action. If asking yourself these questions is not effective, give them to a trusted friend or adviser and have them ask you.

Most people who visualize the miracle find their minds going from the impossible to the possible. Suddenly, even just imagining that this dream or goal is possible broadens your mind, fills your body with positive emotions, and builds important psychological resources to move you forward. The shift can be surprisingly quick.

Confidence Habits

- Find at least five role models and mentors who can help you take your skills and talents to higher levels.
- Do not compare yourself with others. Learn as much as you can from others about how they became successful at exactly what you want to do.
- Create or join a mastermind group to keep the encouragement coming and to keep that confidence muscle strong.
- Picture both the process and the outcome when visualizing.
- Use the miracle questions to boost your self-efficacy when you're feeling particularly hopeless or down.

9

Surround Yourself with the Right People

• • • • •

AN IMPORTANT SOURCE of self-efficacy is knowing that others are encouraging us and giving us the moral support we need, especially when the going gets tough. Pursuing your big goals can take time, and finding strength in the supportive words of others can be extremely helpful.

One of the most significant things I have done is surround myself with a tribe of people who regularly offer me advice, and guide and encourage me. When you are working on making your big goals come true, you need people who will regularly give you a positive boost and tell you "You can do it!" Now, you don't just want cheerleaders who say you are Queen of the Hill, no matter what you do. If people around you raise your confidence unrealistically and you fail at your endeavor, you may never believe their praise again, and their encouragement will fall on deaf ears in the future. Constructive and realistic feedback that focuses on your capabilities will raise efficacy beliefs.

Research shows that feedback that focuses on our progress toward a desired goal enhances our beliefs in our personal capabilities, whereas feedback that focuses on gaps between you and the goal highlights our weaknesses and does not raise our self-efficacy. In other words, the feedback "Good job. You are 60 percent of the way there!" is more beneficial than "Good job. Only 40 percent to go!"

Research also shows that when people are overly critical of our performance and make disparaging comments, our feelings of self-efficacy are lowered, whereas constructive criticism can boost self-efficacy. The next time someone tries to embarrass you with disparaging feedback or name calling, let them know that you are doing your best to improve and that instructive feedback about exactly what you can do to improve would be much more helpful. Train those around you to do just that.

Find Accountability Partners

Whenever I am embarking on a big goal, I enlist the support of an accountability partner. So many people go through a planning process, set goals for the coming year, and then never revisit them. If you want to achieve your goals, you need to have them top of mind, and you need to be accountable to someone. An accountability partner is someone who is clear about your goal and knows when you want to accomplish it by. They may regularly follow up with you to ensure you are meeting the timeline. Other accountability partners might show up differently. For example, I wanted to start exercising every day and eating right, so I began to check in with like-minded friends at the end of each day, to share what we ate and the exercise we engaged in. Because I knew I had to report at the end of the day, I was motivated to eat right and do my exercise in order not to be embarrassed in front of my peers. We also encouraged each other and helped each other stay on track, especially after setbacks. Being accountable to someone who is both friendly and firm can push you past the fear and procrastination toward completion of your goals.

Hire a Coach

If you are finding it difficult to surround yourself with encouraging people, you might want to hire a coach to help you raise your confidence and keep you on track for your goals. Coaches are in the business of helping you succeed and are trained to help you learn, gain clarity, and stay focused on measurable progress. According to the International Coach Federation, clients reported that their productivity and work performance improved by using a coach. Clients also reported higher levels of self-confidence, improved relationships, improved communication skills, and improved work-life balance.[44]

I have hired many coaches over the years. When people say to me that they can't afford a coach, I always respond that sometimes you need to spend money to make money. Every coach I have worked with has helped me significantly boost my revenue, making it worth the investment. Coaches are also trained to spot negative ways of thinking and guide you toward more productive thinking. Surrounding yourself with positive people, having accountability partners, and hiring a coach are all good sources of regular encouragement, but you also need to be aware of how negative people you associate with may be influencing your behavior.

The Pygmalion Effect

You may recall from chapter 4 the discussion of the Pygmalion effect, the phenomenon whereby our beliefs become self-fulfilling prophecies. Did you know that even other people's beliefs about you can become self-fulfilling prophecies? Social persuasion can have a powerful effect, even when people don't come right out and say something to discourage us. In the 1960s, Robert Rosenthal, a researcher at Harvard University, tested the power of other people's expectations on our behaviors by conducting a revolutionary study in the classroom.[45] At the beginning of the year, he administered a nonverbal IQ test to students in eighteen classrooms at the elementary level. Based on the results of the test, he then informed teachers who the "intellectual bloomers" were, indicating that they would improve markedly in comparison with the other students. The teachers were instructed to not tell the students this and just continue to teach the way they would normally. When he tested the same group of children eight months later, he found that the IQ of these students had increased considerably more than that of the children in the control group.

What the teachers did not know, however, is that those students had been chosen *completely at random* and then the researchers labeled those children as intellectual bloomers. So what happened? Researchers believe that when a certain expectation is set in someone's mind, they look for things that are consistent with that expectation. So, for example, if a teacher knows that Johnny has been identified as an intellectual bloomer, perhaps she overlooks his errors in class or gives him extra attention. She may think, *Oh, Johnny's just having a bad day today; he actually is an intellectual bloomer*. Another reason could be that the student themselves pick up on subtle cues from their teachers and are encouraged to do better—we are highly sensitive to feedback, praise, and criticism.

Researchers also believe that when we have certain expectations of people, we send them messages with our body language, called "micro-expressions." Sometimes we're not even aware that we are sending these micro-messages. Our expectations of others are communicated either directly or indirectly (through our body language), and the other person then fulfills that expectation. If we believe our teachers have more faith in us, we step up our efforts. Our teachers' beliefs help us create self-fulfilling prophecies. The Harvard experiment has been replicated several times over the years, and in the workplace too, with the same results.

So be careful whom you hang around with! Just being in the presence of a group of naysayers, even if they don't verbalize, can affect you. I'm not saying you have to isolate yourself and stay away from any and all negative sources. Naysayers may have interesting or important information that can ultimately help you. I'm just saying that they may be having an effect on you, and you need to protect your feelings of confidence.

The Only Validation You Need Is Your Own

In my experience, the people who can sometimes be the most discouraging and who often rain on your parade are family members. For some reason, they think they have the right and the obligation to tell you how stupid your ideas are. Possibly it's meant to save you from ultimate doom or to prevent you from achieving greater success than them—there's a pecking order in some families, and everyone must maintain their original standing. Who are you to shine brighter than you are today?

The problem is that receiving negative feedback from family members is more troubling than when it comes from nonfamily members—no matter how old we are, we are always seeking the validation of those we love most, especially our parents. It's as though we revert to our childhood, wanting validation from our parents.

For years, I wanted my mother and father to validate my success, something they were never really able to do. At one point, I ran into a friend of my mother's, who said, "You know, I don't think your mother knows what you do for a living." It was true. Both my mother and father never took much of an interest in my career. So I gave up on seeking this validation. I stopped telling them about my successes because every time I did, they would just say, "That's nice" and quickly move on to another topic. It felt like they were ignoring the accomplishment, and I would be disappointed. One time my father even asked me if I actually got paid for what I do. I don't want to give you the wrong impression of my parents. They were wonderful, caring individuals who loved me to the moon and back, and I loved them both dearly too. They just weren't big on validating my accomplishments.

I think that sometimes our parents' reaction is meant to be protective. Perhaps, if they don't think it is a good idea for you to move forward with an idea, they want to prevent you from being hurt. They want to do everything possible to prevent you from feeling bad. Once I recognized this instinct in my parents, I could anticipate exactly how they would react to my ideas and business endeavors. I also recognized that they weren't trying to hurt me.

Everyone is entitled to their opinion. But just because someone doesn't believe in you, that doesn't mean you have to change your course of action. My parents were projecting their self-doubt on me. Once I knew how they would react, their reaction stopped having such an impact on me. I realized that they did not know any other way to show up. So every time they gave me feedback, I'd just say, "Thank you so much for your consideration. I'll think about that." And then I would move on to the next topic.

I finally convinced myself of this important message: *You do not need your parents' validation to do this. Period. You only need your own.*

If you are constantly seeking external validation, you will always be at the mercy of others. Take control of your own drive and reasons for moving forward with your dreams and find the tribe that will share this journey with you. It is a wonderful moment when you decide you don't need validation of your dreams in order to go and live them.

Speaking of parents, the kind of criticism and praise you received as a child may have a greater influence on your confidence and may have a much greater impact on your willingness to act than you may think. It can also have lingering effects on how you think, behave, and feel well into adulthood. In fact, these lingering beliefs can affect your entire mindset.

Do You Have a Fixed or a Growth Mindset?

According to Stanford psychologist and researcher Dr. Carol Dweck, people have one of two kinds of mindsets when approaching challenges: fixed or growth.[46] Those with a fixed mindset believe that their intelligence or talent is determined early in life. Either you're born smart or talented, or you're not. People with a growth mindset believe that their intelligence or talent can be increased and improved with practice, training, and effort. In other words, you're not just born with it.

According to Dr. Dweck, certain kinds of feedback, especially from parents, teachers, and leaders, can create a particular mindset. You might think that all praise we give to someone will have a positive effect on performance, but Dr. Dweck discovered otherwise. Praising people using "person praise" instead of "process praise" can foster a fixed mindset, which ultimately results in nonproductive responses after setbacks. Person praise focuses on ability, intelligence, talent, or goodness after performing a task and involves a global evaluation of the person. For example, saying "You are a genius" after an achievement praises the person for being intelligent. Now that person is attributing their achievement to the fixed trait of being intelligent. The more person praise someone receives, the more he or she will believe that intelligence or talent is fixed, developing a fixed mindset.

Feedback that focuses on a person's strategies, hard work, or efforts—process praise—fosters a growth mindset that produces mastery-oriented responses to setbacks, which is exactly what you want if you are trying to build your competence and confidence. For example, saying "You must have worked really hard on that" praises the process. Now the person believes his or her accomplishments are attributed to hard work. It's not a fixed trait anymore, so the person is motivated to work harder and increase the likelihood of success.

When I was a kid, I was always put in the "smart" group at school, regardless of what grade I was in. From Grade 1 to Grade 8, I never moved into another group, and neither did anyone else in my class. I was always told how smart I was. After a while, I developed a fixed mindset. This was problematic for me because I was always worried about making mistakes in front of others. Mistakes made me look stupid (I believed), and I didn't like that feeling. So over the years, either I didn't engage in anything that would challenge my intelligence or I'd be filled with huge anxiety when I did go after certain goals, always worried I would not measure up to my self-view. When I suffered a setback, my self-image was put into question, and I would engage in self-sabotaging behaviors to protect my self-worth. For example, if I thought a certain endeavor was leading to failure, I would give up or quit before I failed, so as not to risk looking stupid in front of my peers. I carried this fixed mindset well into my adult years. It wasn't until I read Dr. Dweck's research that I learned how to shift from a fixed mindset to a growth mindset. And when I did, it was life-altering.

Change Your Mindset

The main reason it is important to understand and shift a fixed mindset to a growth mindset is that the latter can have profound effects on your behavior, motivation, and feelings. A fixed mindset can deter you from engaging in challenging endeavors, especially if you think you might fail, whereas a growth mindset allows you to more readily engage in success behaviors, *even* if you think you might fail.

Let's first explore how a fixed mindset might hold someone back. The main goal for someone with a fixed mindset is to look good. The focus is on the end result and how it will positively reinforce their self-image. Much of their behavior is driven by a desire to protect their self-image. If they see themselves as intelligent, they are focused on how the end result will reinforce how intelligent they are. As a result, those with a fixed mindset:

1. **Avoid challenges.** If they are not sure they can master the task or be successful, then showing off their intelligence is in jeopardy. What if they fail? Then people might think they are not smart anymore. If a fixed mindset motivates people to avoid challenges, how will they ever be able to take their skills to the next level?

2. **Give up easily when faced with obstacles.** Once again, obstacles put success at risk. Obstacles also offer a great cover story when they are not succeeding—they can blame the obstacle, not their lack of intelligence or talent.

3. **Don't put in the required effort.** Those with a fixed mindset see effort as a sign of unintelligence. If they have to try really hard and expend a great deal of effort, they must not be that smart. That is the message those with a fixed mindset hears when the going gets tough.

4. **Avoid listening to constructive criticism.** When given an opportunity to receive valuable criticism that might help future performance, those with a fixed mindset shy away. Criticism only makes them look and feel bad.

5. **Are jealous of the success of others.** When others are performing better than they are, they feel bad because their focus is on looking good. When we are jealous of the success of others, we resent them and do not approach them for valuable success information.

6. **Perform worse.** Researchers discovered that those with a fixed mindset performed worse compared with those in the

When you reach the end of your rope, tie a knot and hang on.

BIANCA OCCHIPINTI (AKA MY MOTHER)

growth-mindset group doing the same task. Researchers believe that people with a fixed mindset may be reluctant to try new strategies when the going gets tough.

After reading this list of behaviors of the fixed mindset, I thought, *Oh my God, I have a fixed mindset!* I shied away from challenges that didn't make me look intelligent or talented. I was jealous of my colleagues' successes. I thought there was something wrong with me because I was always putting in a ton of effort, which made me feel untalented. I was crushed when I failed in front of others, ruminating about it for days.

Do you have a fixed mindset? Do you recognize any of your own behaviors in the list above? Can you see how a fixed mindset might be holding you back? It's okay if you do, because there are ways to shift your mindset. Since a growth mindset helps you achieve greater success, let's explore this perspective in detail, to see how your mindset can affect six critical elements of success.

The Growth Mindset

People with a growth mindset are much more concerned with how the task at hand will help them learn, grow, or stretch. As long as the endeavor helps them progress, they will engage in it. Thus, the goals they set are learning goals. As a result, those with a growth mindset:

1. **Embrace challenge.** They know that pushing their skills to the next challenging level will help them learn and grow.

They are not focused on the end performance, only on whether the experience will help them learn and grow, and they are not too concerned about how they look in the process. The challenge motivates them because they know it's taking their talent to a higher level.

2 **Persist in the face of obstacles.** Obstacles are seen as challenges to be overcome, not barriers to success. Once again, the goal is to grow, so they learn from the setback and then try again. Because those with a growth mindset are not focused on the end result, the setback does not affect them as much as it would those with a fixed mindset; they are paying attention on how to improve their performance in the next try.

3 **See effort as the path to mastery.** Effort is a sign they are on the right track. Effort is what is required to succeed, and if they are not succeeding, they haven't worked hard enough. My ex-husband, who has a growth mindset, wants to always be the worst player at his level in his squash league. That way, every player he challenges is better than him, and he can learn and grow with each game. He usually works very hard to make his way up the ladder, and once he's near the top, he asks to be moved to the next level, where he can start at the bottom once again.

4 **Learn from criticism.** Those with a growth mindset are open to listening and incorporating the learning that comes from effective feedback, which allows them to do better the next time. Criticism is welcome because it helps them reach mastery sooner.

5 **Find inspiration in the success of others.** Instead of feeling jealous for others' success, those with a growth mindset draw inspiration from others who are better at the task than they are.

6 **Perform better.** Those with a growth mindset do better on tasks compared with those with a fixed mindset, and also enjoy themselves in the process. Perhaps it is because they are not so worried about whether they fail or succeed—less worry translates into better focus on performing well. They are also more inclined to try new strategies when tried strategies are not working.

Developing a growth mindset can be critical to recovering from setbacks and continuing to build your competence.

After learning about Dr. Dweck's work, I realized that if I wanted to break through my current level of success and go after my biggest goals, I would have to learn how to have a growth mindset. I had to shift from focusing on looking good to focusing on learning and growing. The first thing I knew I had to do was start caring less about what other people thought about me and more about developing my talent, even if it was a rocky road to the top. But how can you go from being worried all the time about how others perceive you to not caring so much? That moment came for me while I was lying in a hospital bed.

In November 2011, I was working very hard on organizing the first CPPA conference, which was to be held in July 2012. I was questioning everything about myself and was so stressed out, there were weeks when my heart would be pounding the entire day. I have never felt that kind of prolonged stress. I was exercising regularly, and one day had a muscle cramp in my leg. I couldn't recall doing anything out of the ordinary. But the cramp didn't go away, like a muscle cramp usually does after a few days.

That week I was at a party, where I saw my girlfriend Sue. Sue is psychic. Yes, I really mean that. She's been my friend since I was thirteen years old, and she has predicted the freakiest things. She shocks me sometimes. So that night I complained to her about the muscle cramp, and she said, "Louisa, that's not a muscle cramp. That pain in your leg is from the birth control you're on. You need to go to the doctor and get that checked out immediately." Then I thought, *Yeah, it is weird that it's been several days and the pain isn't going away... and the label on the birth control does say risk of blood clots... risk of death... And also, how the hell does Sue know my gynecologist put me on birth control to manage my crazy hormones? I never told her that.*

On Monday morning, I called my gynecologist's office. I left a message but my call wasn't returned. So the next day I thought, *Maybe I should just go the hospital...* And then it hit me. I felt like I was having a heart attack... I couldn't breathe... my lungs felt like they were collapsing. My husband rushed me to Emergency. They brought me right in and ran ECGs, MRIs, blood tests, and ultrasounds. After what seemed like hours of testing, the doctor came to talk to me. He looked at me solemnly and said, "Louisa, as you know, we have run a number of tests, and we did find evidence of something serious."

Something serious? But I'm sitting here responding to emails. How serious can it be? The doctor continued. "I'm afraid you have had a pulmonary embolism. That's when a blood clot in your body breaks off and travels through your bloodstream and then gets caught in your lungs. Most people die from pulmonary embolisms—if they are big enough, they cut off oxygen flow to the heart. You are very lucky that yours were small and did not cause too much damage. You were very, very lucky, Louisa."

Silence.

I had almost died.

I could be dead right now.

Dead.

I suddenly thought about all the things I hadn't done yet. I was always too afraid to put myself out there because I thought that no one would be interested in what I had to say. I was never smart enough or had the right academic credentials. I made a decision that day that as I embarked on my next level in my life and what I was passionate about, looking bad in front of others was no longer going to be an obstacle for me. Once I did that, I realized that people didn't really care about my setbacks. Most people were excited about my progress. When people tried to tear me down, I smiled at them and then *I ignored them*. I stayed focused on all those people I was serving and kept learning how I could serve them better and better. I focused on the value I brought to people who wanted me to succeed. Instead of focusing on looking good, which is a fixed-mindset behavior, I focused on learning, which developed my growth-mindset muscles.

Always focusing on the naysayers and how to live up to their standard just makes you better at serving the naysayers, who will never be on your side. You could bring them lattes every morning, mow their lawn, and shower them with gifts—they're still never going to change. Instead, by focusing on the people who truly love what you do and figuring out how to serve them better, more and more people will want to follow you because you deliver exceptional value. With this attitude, I was able to build a following of thousands of people.

I'm not perfect, and I'm not aiming for perfect. I'm just doing the best I can. We have to start caring less about what other people think about us. Don't wait until you are in a hospital bed to figure this out. None of us knows when our last day will be.

The Power of Yet

In an interview, I asked Dr. Dweck what her most powerful tool was for shifting from a fixed mindset to a growth mindset. She says it's the power of "yet." Every time you are putting yourself down and perhaps saying something like "I'm not good at math," add "yet" to the end of the statement: "I'm not good at math *yet*" or "I'm not a great nurse *yet*." Go ahead and try this for yourself. Can you just feel the shift of energy with the addition of just one powerful word? Keep "yet" handy and use it whenever you feel you are not good enough.

This next exercise will help you feel good about your own standards and worry less about the standards set by others.

EXERCISE: **ELIMINATING "SHOULD" FROM YOUR LIFE**

Years ago, I would often compare myself with others or care more about what other people thought, and I would place impossible standards on myself. These kind of self-judgments showed up as "should" statements, which zapped my energy, confidence, and happiness.

I believe "should" statements are the enemy of all women. Do any of these sound familiar to you?

I should be further along in my life by now.

I should eat better.

I should exercise more.

I should spend more time with my kids.

I should have more sex.

My home should be cleaner.

I should be making more money.

I should visit my mother more often.

All these statements are really just standards that have been set by us, by society, or by our parents to demonstrate how we don't measure up for some reason. "Should" statements usually come from guilt; something like: *If I were a better person, I would go see my mom more often.* "Should" statements are also an expression of your feeling you are not good enough, and an excellent meal for our self-doubt monsters. When you say "should," you are implying that there is a goal that you're not meeting. "Should" statements are a great way to beat yourself up. It is time to eliminate "should" from our vocabulary and instead use "want."

Step 1

You will need a small pad of sticky notes. Sit in a quiet place and contemplate all the things you are "shoulding" about. Write down each "should" statement, one per note. Once you believe you have written them all down, arrange them in a column on a table.

Now take a look. Reflect on them. In your journal, write down how you are feeling when you sit in these "should" statements. Below or on a separate page, write down what you feel like doing right now. Notice where in your body you are feeling it. Do you feel productive or defeated? Give yourself time to fully understand what these statements are doing to your body, brain, and motivation. It doesn't feel good does it?

Step 2

Now take a look at each "should" statement and ask yourself, *What do I want instead?* Beside each "should" statement, write the corresponding "want" statement. For example, using the list above:

"Should" Statement	**"Want" Statement**
I should be further along in my life by now.	I want to feel good about my accomplishments to date.
I should eat better.	I want to eat nutritious food as much as I can.
I should exercise more.	I want to get out into nature and move for an hour every day.
I should spend more time with my kids.	I want to spend quality time with my kids.
I should have more sex.	I want to have intimate moments with my husband several times a week.
My home should be cleaner.	I want my home to be a peaceful place I come to at the end of the day.
I should be making more money.	I want to feel financially secure.
I should visit my mother more often.	I want to see my mother at least once a week.

Now contemplate your "want" statements and contrast how they make you feel, as opposed to reading the "should" statements. Can you feel the positive shift in energy?

Step 3

Now take all your "should" statements, crumple each one up into a ball, and throw them all in the recycling bin. Commit to never "shoulding" on yourself again and to eliminating "should" from your vocabulary. The next time you hear yourself "shoulding," stop and ask yourself, *What do I want instead?*

Aah. Now, doesn't that feel good?

Step 4

Now look at all the things you want in your life. Beside each want, think about one or two you would like to prioritize. Don't go after all at once, as that is just a recipe for failure. Making a commitment to something takes mental energy. If you take on too many things at once, you will not have the mental resources to commit to it all. It is better to just focus on one or two things that are really important to you right now. It doesn't mean you don't think the others are important, but you can get to them later. So, looking at one or two wants, think about strategies you could put into place to help you incorporate these wants into your life. Who could help you with these?

For example, "I want to get out into nature and move for an hour every day." I have a dog walker who walks my dog when I go into the office. I decided to let the dog walker go, and I started bringing my dog into work. Every day over the lunch hour, I take her out for a long stroll. At the end of the day, we go to Sherwood Park, a lovely place near my home, and my dog and I enjoy another long walk in the forest there. This has now become one of the most enjoyable times of my day.

Write down as many strategies as you can think of. Talk them over with friends and see if they have further ideas. When we sit in our "should"s all the time, we are constantly at the whim of what everyone else thinks our standards should be. When we set our own goals for ourselves, and not to please others, we can show up more authentically in our lives. It takes confidence to decide that whatever goals you set for yourself are good enough. But once you do, life will unfold exactly as you wish.

Confidence Habits

- Surround yourself with positive, uplifting people. Messages of encouragement and support are more important to building self-efficacy than you may think.
- Understand that we are very sensitive to subtle cues, so even if naysayers don't verbalize a thought, they may be subconsciously discouraging you. Know your genuine tribe.
- Hire a coach if you can't find encouraging people to surround yourself with.
- Nurture a growth mindset by focusing on how you are going to learn and grow from each experience, rather than focusing on merely looking good.
- Care less about what other people think about you but be open to constructive feedback.
- Stop holding yourself to impossible standards by replacing "should" with "want."

10

Use Your Body and Emotions as Power

A FINAL SOURCE OF self-efficacy is our body and emotional states. We often believe that our body reacts to our thoughts and emotions—that it's a one-way street. What is less commonly known is that our bodily states, also known as somatic states, contribute to our feelings of confidence. As well, our emotions—whether triggered by some event or by emotions that are present because of our current mood—can influence our feelings of confidence. It is not so much the states or the emotions itself that contribute but the meaning we place on these states and emotions that will influence our feelings of self-confidence. In this chapter we explore three pathways to greater confidence: bodily states, emotional triggers, and overall moods.

Bodily States

I had the pleasure of interviewing Dr. Kate Hefferon, reader of psychology at the University of East London, who specializes in the somatic side of well-being: how our physical selves and perception of our physical selves affect our thinking and influence our well-being and confidence. The scientific term for what she studies is the somatopsychic principle, which is linked to a new area of research, "embodied cognition," that is getting a lot of interest in psychology these days. Scientists are starting to discover that our bodily states, our environment, and the actions we engage in all influence what we think. And everything we think, see, or feel is mediated via our body, so it is important to recognize our body as a potential means of perception. Scientists have discovered that when we manipulate our body into a more confident pose, like sitting up straight rather than slouching, we are sometimes likely to have greater confidence in our abilities and traits.

Power Poses

Amy Cuddy, Caroline Wilmuth, and Dana Carney, all of Harvard University, ran an experiment to see if standing in certain "power poses" *before* a high-stakes performance would improve subsequent performance of the task.[47] Participants were asked to adopt an expansive pose, such as hands high in the air or hands on the hips (i.e., Wonder Woman pose) for two minutes, and then prepare and deliver a speech to two evaluators as part of a mock job interview. As predicted, high-power posers performed better. The high-power posers were able to better maintain their composure, project more confidence, and present more captivating and enthusiastic speeches, which led to higher performance evaluations and a higher likelihood of being chosen for hire.

Power posing could have helped participants effectively prepare for the speech by boosting their psychological power, which has been shown to enhance performance. When giving a speech, we can sometimes feel powerless because it is one person (us) being evaluated by many. By engaging in power poses before the delivery, participants can shift those feelings of power, build confidence, and subsequently improve performance. Overall, power posing is a new area of research, with room for further explanation, replication, and development, but many studies have shown effects on subjective feelings of power.[48]

Physical Activity

When I asked Dr. Hefferon for the best embodied intervention for boosting confidence, she told me that, without a doubt, it's physical activity. In fact, "physical activity and being active is one of the most important things we can do for our physical and psychological health," she said. "It can reduce anxiety and depression, and produce positive outcomes such as higher self-esteem and positive emotions." Engaging in physical activity increases confidence because we are learning new skills and we have evidence that we have achieved something. I can testify to that: after I finish my morning yoga, I feel good about myself because I have accomplished my goal of exercise for the day. As we are physically active, we gain mastery over our physical self, and this contributes to feelings of confidence. According to Dr. Hefferon, these feelings of confidence transfer to other domains in our lives. Physical activity also makes us feel better about our body.

Positive Body Image

Body image affects our confidence, especially in women. Women need to understand that not having a negative body image is not the same as having a positive body image. That is, it is not enough to say "I don't hate my body." We have to learn to say "I love my body." When we feel good about our body, we feel more positive emotion.

Dr. Hefferon suggests doing three things to boost positive body image. First, ask yourself, *What can my body do well?* Focus on the *functionality* of it, such as your ability to produce children or walk up a flight of stairs or run a marathon. Focusing on the functionality of our body can contribute to a positive body image. Second, *focus on your assets*. In other words, ask yourself, *What parts of my body do I love?* I love my hair, for example. Every time I go to my hairdresser, she says, "Louisa, when God was giving out hair, you were at the front of the line!" I'm not trying to be conceited here; I am merely giving myself permission to say good things about my favorite physical asset.

Gratitude is a third pathway to feeling good about your body. For example, every time I go for a walk through the forest in my neighborhood, I thank God that my feet and legs function perfectly. I have a friend who has such advanced arthritis in his feet that he can no longer go for long walks, something he loved to do. Being grateful for what you can do can be a positive-body-image booster.

We women are so quick to criticize our bodies. We are so inundated with media images of thin, flawless women that it is hard not to judge ourselves. Amy Schumer, a popular comedian and actress, makes fun of the way everyone in LA is so skinny that they mistake her arms for her legs. We all laugh at her jokes but meanwhile, while standing in front of the mirror, we stress about how fat our arms look in that dress.

According to Dr. Hefferon, people who have a positive body image are able to filter out negativity that is presented to them through media images and the external world. Thus, a positive image acts like a protective filter that stops us from comparing ourselves with the highly digitally altered bodies we see in the magazines. She also suggests that everyone be educated about the extent to which media sources and advertisers go to manipulate pictures, producing images that are completely misaligned with reality. The more we know about how unrealistic these images are, the more comfortable we may feel about ourselves.

I recently started CrossFit to feel stronger in my body and have found that it is having a huge effect on my feelings of confidence. Do not underestimate how powerful your body can make you feel.

Emotional Triggers

Judgments about our level of confidence can be influenced by the emotions that are triggered when we think about performing an upcoming task. If, for example, I experience anxiety and stress every time I contemplate writing an exam, this may be a cue to my brain that I am about to fail and this, in turn, can lower my self-efficacy about passing the exam. Similarly, if I walk into the exam room and my heart starts racing and I start perspiring, this may send a message to my brain that I am about to fail. This may then trigger a stress reaction that has detrimental effects on my performance on the exam, which is the exact opposite of what I want to happen! Again, it is important to note that it's not the bodily state or emotion itself that interferes with one's performance; it is the interpretation of what those physical messages mean. If you start perspiring and you ascribe your sweat to the room being too warm, this may not affect your self-efficacy at all. If you feel anxious but are able to tell yourself, *Everyone gets nervous before a big exam. It's normal,* your self-efficacy may not be affected. Thus, the impact these messages have on your self-efficacy will vary depending on the situation and the meaning you give to them.

I recently had a big speaking engagement for which I bought a new dress. I decided to wear Spanx underneath it—Spanx are body-shaping undergarments that kind of suck everything in, for a slimming effect. When I entered the ballroom to give my presentation, I found myself short of breath. At first I thought it was a sign of my anxiety and I grew nervous, but when I got curious about how I was feeling, I realized it was the Spanx! Those things felt like they were cutting off oxygen to my lungs, and I was finding it hard to breathe! Hilarious what we do to look good. Once I was able to reinterpret my physiological state, my nervousness went away and my confidence was restored.

The next time you are feeling nervous or anxious and as a result begin to perspire or find yourself short of breath before a big performance, see if you can put new labels on how you are feeling. Maybe you can interpret nervousness as focused attention, shift anxiety into excitement, fear into exhilaration, or anger into being "fired up." By putting a new label on the feeling, you may improve your self-efficacy and confidence. I had a friend who was going to give a TEDx Talk and was extremely nervous about it. Every time she practiced, she would start shaking. When she realized that being nervous while delivering a TEDx is totally normal (who *isn't* nervous giving one?!) and that shaking on camera would not be a big deal, she stopped feeling so nervous and began to relax. Being in a relaxed state helped her perform better.

There are times when I do feel nervous before a big talk, so one of the best tools I use to remove the feelings of nervousness is taking three very long breaths. I take at least eight counts to inhale and eight counts to exhale. This stimulates my parasympathetic nervous system, which triggers a calming response in my body. After just three slow inhales and exhales, I find I am much calmer and ready to go.

Overall Mood

When you're in a great mood, don't you feel confident? I do. I feel like I can achieve anything when I'm feeling happy. According to research, we actually do experience greater self-efficacy when we are in a good mood—and we experience lowered self-efficacy when in a bad mood.

Here's how it works. Researchers believe that emotions act like a mental filter through which people view and interpret events that can subsequently affect self-efficacy. According to some theories, past successes and failures are stored as memories, along with the emotions they carried. So if I asked you to recall a happy event in your life, not only will you recall the event but you may also feel the emotions you had when you experienced that event. A past success would be stored in your memory, along with the associated emotions of excitement, confidence, and happiness. A happy mood might trigger positive memories of previous successes and past accomplishments, positively impacting self-efficacy in the present moment, whereas a negative mood might induce thoughts of past failures.

A depressed mood may also activate a global view of oneself as inadequate, which may increase self-doubt and lower feelings of confidence. This may cause a downward spiral in the sense that feelings of depression can lower self-efficacy, which reduces motivation, which breeds poor performance, which makes us feel even more depressed. In contrast, a good mood raises efficacy beliefs, which fuels motivation, which stimulates better performance and achievement, which, once again, makes us feel even better. So if you want to stay confident and fuel those feelings of confidence, it will be important to manage your mood.

Women, Depression, and Rumination

Managing one's emotional state is important, especially for women. Regardless of the country they live in, women are twice as likely as men to experience major depression. This statistic concerns me, because I know how negative emotional states can undermine confidence. I wondered why women were twice as likely to suffer from depression as men are.

The late Dr. Susan Nolen-Hoeksema, a researcher at Yale University, was dedicated to determining why women were more prone to depression. Over the years, many hypotheses were put forward, but one behavior stood out in the research as the number one contributor to female depression: rumination.[49]

Rumination is overthinking a past situation or life event and dwelling on it. These constant repetitive thoughts—thinking about something over and over—keep you stuck in the problem, perpetuating negative thoughts and emotions, as well as feelings of hopelessness. Several long-term studies show that people who ruminate in response to stress have an increased risk of major depression.

Research shows that women have a more emotional ruminative coping style than men do when dealing with stressful situations. They tend to focus inward on feelings rather than outward on taking action to change their situations. People who ruminate when they are stressed typically have longer periods of depression than those who do not ruminate, which could put them at risk for developing other psychological disorders over time. Rumination has also been linked to anxiety, binge eating, binge drinking, and self-harm.

It is important to control rumination if you want to maintain your confidence and manage your emotional state—and it's possible to stop ruminating by implementing techniques described in this book. I also wrote a short ebook on how to stop ruminating, called *The Rumination Cure*. You can download it for free at http://louisajewell.com/the-rumination-cure.

Managing Your Daily Mood by Managing Your Positivity Ratio

Since maintaining a positive mood is an important contributor to feelings of self-efficacy, I want to share my favorite exercise, which, for the past six years, has dramatically changed my daily experience and significantly helped me to manage my mood.

When you are trying to lose weight, you put yourself on a diet of healthy food and try to stay away from salt-and-vinegar potato chips and chocolate cake. It is the same when you are trying to manage your daily mood. Negative emotions can spark a downward spiral, whereas positive emotions can spark an upward spiral. If you recall from chapter 6, our brain has what is called a negativity bias. Thus, we need to experience many more positive emotions than negative emotions in our day in order to maintain a happy mood.

Look at all the emotions you experience during a day. Positive emotions are things like love, gratitude, joy, excitement, pride, serenity, and awe. Negative emotions are things like anger, disappointment, frustration, anxiety, jealousy, and sadness. Your positivity ratio is the number of positive emotions divided by the number of negative emotions you experience in your day.

$$\frac{\text{Number of positive emotions}}{\text{Number of negative emotions}} = \text{Your positivity ratio}$$

You can fail at what you don't want, so you might as well take a chance at doing what you love.

I first heard of the concept of a positivity ratio from Dr. Barbara Fredrickson, a leading researcher in the study of positive emotions.[50] She outlined the research in neuroscience that supports the idea that people achieve higher levels of flourishing when they are experiencing positivity ratios of approximately 3, 4, or 5 to 1. Higher ratios correlated with flourishing, whereas low ratios correlated with feelings of depression.[51]

I started monitoring my ratio in 2008, with the intention of increasing it every day. The results were incredible. My mood was better, my energy was much higher, and my confidence went way up. Dr. Fredrickson's research shows that positive emotions broaden our thinking and build important physical, social, and psychological resources that actually fuel greater productivity and motivation.

Some people confuse positive emotions with positive thinking. Positive emotions are feelings you have in your body that make you feel good, whereas positive thinking is looking on the bright side of things. Sometimes when we talk about the positivity ratio, some people think we are asking people to always be optimistic and only look at the good. I am not asking you to think positively all the time. That is not realistic. You can look at all the downsides and upsides of something while still cultivating positive emotion. For example, say I am an attorney cross-examining someone on the stand who is accused of a crime and my questions are incriminating him. I am engaged in critical thinking, but feelings of excitement and pride fill my body at the prospect of winning the case. That is an example of positive emotion, as opposed to positive thinking.

The first step in increasing your positivity ratio is to become aware of your emotions throughout the day. What do you do every day to bring yourself moments of positive emotion? What do you do to bring yourself moments of negative emotion? Make note of what you do to introduce these feelings into your day.

For me, actions that brought positive emotions included savoring my morning shower, petting and walking my dog, watching half an hour of my favorite TV comedy show, calling a close girlfriend, hugging my children, eating healthy food, doing hot yoga, doing work I love, being kind to my Tim Hortons server, and expressing gratitude. Once I was aware of these little things, I began to find ways to bring more positive moments into my day.

I also noticed that I engaged in a lot of unnecessary negativity that brought me down. For example, if a driver cut me off on the highway, I would ruminate on it and tell people at the office about it—and I'd still be thinking about it as I went home that night. Ruminating on these minor negative incidents certainly brought my ratio down. I also noticed that the murder mysteries I watched on TV usually were about the brutal murders of women—and I'd have nightmares later about the murders.

This exercise is not about avoiding all negative emotion—I don't think that's possible or healthy. If your daughter is being bullied at school, it's natural to feel angry as you take steps to deal with it. If a friend has just been diagnosed with cancer, you may feel sadness as you lend her your support. It is important that you feel the full range of emotions in your day. So again, it's not about avoiding the negative. It's about letting go of the *unnecessary* negative.

Easier said than done! So I turned to the wisdom of my dear friend David Pollay and his book *The Law of the Garbage Truck: How to Respond to People Who Dump on You and How to Stop Dumping on Others*. David taught me how to recognize the people in my life who walk around filled with garbage, just looking for ways they can dump their garbage on you. Once I recognized it as garbage, I could choose not to engage in their negativity. I no longer allowed them to affect my day. I would say, *That's their garbage, not mine.*

Soon after learning about the Law of the Garbage Truck, I had a minor driving incident. I had come to a three-way stop, then moved forward when it was my turn. But then the traffic stopped and I found myself stuck in the middle of the intersection. Other drivers could still go around me to get by, but my car was definitely in the way. I was waiting patiently for the traffic to advance when a truck entered the intersection. The driver must have seen that there was nowhere I could move to just then, and he could also easily go around my car, but instead he leaned on his horn and yelled at me. I just patiently smiled and waved at him, and shrugged my shoulders as if to say, "Oh well." I did not allow the incident to upset me. I could have easily told the driver off, but I knew that that would be unnecessary negativity. He was dumping his garbage, and I wasn't going to accept it. What was funny is that after his angry display, he drove his truck around me, just like he could have done in the first place. Engaging in unnecessary negativity uses up important psychological energy that you could be using to achieve your goals.

I also began to recognize the garbage I was creating for myself—for example, every time I watched those reality shows where people are yelling at each other, like *Judge Judy*, I was engaging in unnecessary negativity. And every time I got upset about people cutting me off in traffic. Remember, managing your positivity ratio is about increasing the positive and eliminating the *unnecessary* negative.

Now that I've introduced the positivity ratio, it's time to put it to work.

EXERCISE: **POSITIVITY-RATIO CHALLENGE: TAKE ACTION TO INCREASE YOUR POSITIVITY RATIO**

1. Become aware of the things that bring you positive moments in the day. Write down what they are. Make a choice to bring more of these positive experiences into your daily routine. Schedule this into your calendar and make it a priority.

2. Become aware of the activities that bring unnecessary negative emotions into your day. Write down what they are. As you flip through the channels of possible experiences and get to something that will make you feel unnecessarily sad, blue, angry, frustrated, upset, alarmed, or disappointed, you can choose to switch to another channel. Make a choice to

stop engaging in those unnecessary negative experiences. I always ask myself, *Do I need to engage in this?* If it is important to me, then yes. If it is not, then no. It's as simple as that—just decide which emotions you will engage.

3 Try this for two weeks and see how it makes a difference in your life. It needs to be a daily practice in order for you to experience benefits. This practice has changed my life. I hope it has the same effect on you.

Confidence Habits

- Your body posture and bodily states can have an effect on your confidence. Reinterpret any signs of nervousness to boost your confidence.
- Create a positive body image by focusing on your body's functionality and what it can do for you, and by focusing on the parts of your body you love.
- Exercise. It may be the single best thing you can do to maintain your physical and psychological health, boost happiness, and increase confidence.
- Manage your positivity ratio, to help keep you in the positive mental mood you need to feel confident.

Conclusion
Now It's Your Turn

• • • • •

I HAVE GIVEN YOU a powerful formula for confidence. Once you rewire your brain, it feels like the canoe you have been paddling upstream with so much effort has been turned around to float freely with the direction of the river. When you wire your brain for confidence, there is little resistance toward big, scary goals.

Building your confidence muscles takes daily practice. The next time you're contemplating your most desired dreams and goals and you find you're stopping yourself, remember how you can leverage the four major sources of self-efficacy. Here is a recap:

1. **Performance or Mastery Experiences:** The best way to build your self-efficacy is to go out and try it, practice, and learn from every iteration. If you're hesitating, take baby steps to chip away at resistance until your confidence builds.

2. **Vicarious Experiences:** Find role models who inspire and teach you—five, to be exact. Mentally rehearse a successful

performance before you try it. Visualize the process and the desired outcome.

3 **Social Persuasion:** Surround yourself with the most supportive and encouraging people you can and stay away from the naysayers.

4 **Bodily and Emotional States:** Build strength in your body, reinterpret bodily signals that make you feel anxious, and keep yourself in a positive mood.

Believing in yourself is the most important skill you need to move boldly toward your dreams. You have the tools. Now it's your turn to kick self-doubt to the curb and say yes to what you really want in your life.

Now more than ever, we need confidence. If we want a liberated, loving, and compassionate world, we need those with a higher consciousness to make it happen. We need to believe in ourselves and our ability to make change and challenge the status quo. The days of blaming others for what is or is not happening in our lives and in our world are over.

We need not only confidence but *warrior-like* confidence. We need to be warriors who are willing to fight for justice, love, peace, and gender equality. Warriors who are rebellious when required, protectors of what is right and wrong, and ready to fight for truth. We women still have a lot of fighting to do.

We need women with the confidence to rise to the tops of corporations and governments. We need the confidence to start our own businesses and grow them. To do that, we need a commanding presence, a clear sense of identity, the confidence to be tenacious when challenged, and the courage to be successful beyond measure.

We need confidence to be kind and compassionate to ourselves. To be successful without feeling overwhelmed, stressed, and burned-out. We need positive, vibrant energy to joyfully pursue our dreams and live happy lives, because we deserve that.

We need confidence to help others be successful, to know that lighting the path for others will not diminish our own light but bring more light into the world. We need confidence to be a source of inspiration for our tribe and our sisters around the world.

This kind of confidence will not be found in your parents' approval, the applause from an audience, thousands of Facebook "likes," or six-pack abs. This kind of warrior-like confidence can only come from deep within you. Let it be the spark that lights the fire within you. Live every day with the peace and serenity that comes with genuine self-confidence and self-acceptance.

The Time Is Now

Do not wait for someone else to write and sing your song. Only you know the melody of your life, so sing it with your unique voice.

To stand out at work, you cannot shrink when your ideas are challenged. Defend your point of view.

To be an innovator in your field, you need an unshakable faith in your ideas to stand strong in the face of criticism, disapproval, and sometimes ridicule. You can stand strong.

To be a leader at work, in government, and in your community, you need to have the courage to fight for what is right and just, and to inspire those who have put their faith in your leadership. You are a fearless leader.

To be an outstanding entrepreneur, you need to persevere and fight the good fight every day, with joy and passion for what you do. Now go and kick some ass.

To be a creative artist, never be afraid to express who you are. Dare to show the world what you are all about.

To be happy, you need to fully accept and love yourself and to demonstrate that to your loved ones, especially your children. Show yourself compassion every day.

To attract the love you want in your life, you need to feel good about who you are and know that you are always enough.

My wish is that you will do all this joyfully, confidently, and with peace in your heart.

Now go out and rock your world, whatever *you* choose it to be.

I will always be on the sidelines, cheering you on.

Acknowledgments

I ALWAYS KNEW THAT I wanted to write a book. It has been on my bucket list since I can remember, and I talked about it for many years but never got started on it. So I have to say thank you to Geoff Affleck, Marci Shimoff, Janet Attwood, and Chris Attwood for inviting me to their Enlightened Bestseller writing retreat, for it was there that I found the clarity and gained the knowledge I needed to finally sit down and write this book. Thank you for believing in me and showing me that I had an important message to share with the world.

As I began to write, I realized it was harder than I thought. I wish I could tell you it was easy and the words flowed, but that would not be true. So I am so grateful to have had Kathryn Britton as my amazing writing coach. It was Kathryn who, many years before, encouraged me to write my first article for *Positive Psychology News Daily*, and it was Kathryn who lovingly guided and nudged me to write each chapter of this book. Thank you, Kathryn, for never giving up on me and for never allowing me to give up on myself.

I want to thank the many scholars whose work I have referenced in this book and for giving me their time to share their knowledge and improve my understanding of what makes us humans tick. Particularly, I want to thank Patrick Carroll of the Laboratory of the Uncertain Self, Martin Seligman, Jennifer Crocker, Kate Hefferon, Carol Dweck, Sonja Lyubomirsky, Kristin Neff, Robert Biswas-Diener, Fred Luthans, James Maddux, and, of course, Albert Bandura, whose life's work has contributed so much to a better world.

I am so grateful to Jesse Finkelstein and the team at Page Two Strategies, who carried me to the publishing finish line. I especially want to thank Amanda Lewis, my editor, for her patience and grace every time I missed a deadline. It's great to work with an editor who "gets" you and what you want to say, and her contributions to this book were invaluable in shaping what you hold today in your hand.

I am also very grateful to the entire master's of applied positive psychology (MAPP) community and the Canadian Positive Psychology Association (CPPA) community, which continue to feed me great information and are constantly cheering me on, no matter what I am up to. It is those in this tribe who, from the beginning, have been my brothers and sisters on this amazing journey toward learning about and sharing how we can all flourish. There are too many of you to mention, but you know who you are, and to you I am eternally grateful.

To write this book has required those special people who give you hope and the positive energy you need to get back to your keyboard and keep writing. I have to say thank you to

David Pollay, Caroline Miller, and Margarita Tarragona, who, every month for years, listened to my trials and tribulations about the book, offered me a ton of advice and guidance on how to write, publish, and promote the book, and who gave me never-ending words of encouragement. Through my toughest times they have stood steadfast in their support and never let me take my eye off this dream.

I want to say a thank-you to Ann Margetts, who let me hide away at her farm to write this book. It was great to be in her loving energy while I wrote. And I want to thank my family both near and far—in Italy—who have always encouraged me, especially my brother Sal, who would give me the shirt off his back if I asked him to.

Thank you to the women of the book club and to my best friends, who are always ready to lift my spirits with their love, friendship, hugs, food, laughter, dancing, yoga, CrossFit, cheerleading, psychic readings, shoulders to cry on, and positive energy. I am terrified to list you all, for fear that I inadvertently leave someone out, so suffice it to say you know who you are. I love you with all my heart, and I am so very, very blessed to have such an amazing group of women in my tribe. You make my life joyous.

Of all the people who deserve an acknowledgment, my ex-husband, Tim, tops the list. Thank you, Tim, for giving me the space I needed, sometimes going away for weeks at a time to write this book. Thank you also for your constant encouragement and support. Even though we are not together anymore, your friendship and love mean the world to me.

Finally, I want to acknowledge my incredible daughters, Claire and Christina. Despite all my shortcomings as a mother, you have grown up to be women of substance who are not afraid to be authentically true to yourselves. I am so proud of the women you have become, and I am so privileged, every day, to be your mom. I hope one day you will read this book and that it inspires you to live your greatest life—the life you deserve.

Notes

1 International Labour Office Geneva. (n.d.). Small change, big changes: Women and microfinance. http://www.ilo.org/wcmsp5/groups/public/---dgreports/---gender/documents/meetingdocument/wcms_091581.pdf

2 Sandberg, S. (2013). *Lean in: Women, work, and the will to lead* (1st ed.). New York: Alfred A. Knopf).

3 Women in the workforce: Canada. (2016, May 6). Retrieved from http://www.catalyst.org/knowledge/women-workforce-canada#footnote25_5550qqi

4 Chenier, L., & Wohlbold, E. (2011, August 30). Women in senior management: Where are they? Retrieved from http://www.conferenceboard.ca/e-library/abstract.aspx?did=4416

5 http://www.marketwatch.com/story/whats-holding-women-back-a-look-at-female-ambition-in-canada-2016-01-11

6 Mirels, H. L., Greblo, P., & Dean, J. B. (2002). Judgmental self-doubt: Beliefs about one's judgmental prowess. *Personality and Individual Differences*, *33*, 741–58.

7 Braslow, M. D., Guerrettaz, J., Arkin, R. M., & Oleson, K. C. (2012). Self-Doubt. *Social and Personality Psychology Compass*, *6*, 470–82, p. 473.

8 Rich Feller, past president of the National Career Development Association, keynote address at Cannexus conference, Ottawa, Ontario, January 20, 2014.

9 Carroll, P. J., Arkin, R. M., & Shade, C. (2011). Possible selves and self-doubt: A poverty of desired possibility. *Journal of Social Psychological and Personality Science*, *2*(2), 190–98.

10 Stevenson, B., & Wolfers, J. (2009). The paradox of declining female happiness. *American Economic Journal: Economic Policy*, *1*(2), 190–225, p. 220.

11 NEDA. (2009, February 26). National Eating Disorder Association unveils powerful & provocative ad campaign. https://www.nationaleatingdisorders.org/press-rom/press-releases/2009-press-releases/national-eating-disorder-association-unveils-powerful-provocative-ad-campaign

12 Medco Health Solutions. (2011). *America's State of Mind Report* examines trends in the "utilization of mental health-related medications among the insured population." http://apps.who.int/medicinedocs/documents/s19032en/s19032en.pdf
13 For more on SDT, visit http://selfdeterminationtheory.org/
14 Ryan, R. M., & Deci, E. L. (2000). Self-determination theory and the facilitation of intrinsic motivation, social development, and well-being. *American Psychologist, 55*(1), 68–78.
15 Eisenberger, N. I., Lieberman, M. D., & Williams, K. D. (2003). Does rejection hurt? An fMRI study of social exclusion. *Science, 302*(5643), 290–92.
16 Arkin, R. M., Oleson, K. C., & Carroll, P. J. (Eds.). (2010). *Handbook of the uncertain self.* New York: Taylor and Francis.
17 Berglas, S., & Jones, E. (1978). Drug choice as a self-handicapping strategy in response to non-contingent success. *Journal of Personality and Social Psychology, 36*, 405–17.
18 Clance, P. R., & Imes, S. A. (1978). The imposter phenomenon in high achieving women: Dynamics and therapeutic intervention. *Psychotherapy: Theory, Research & Practice, 15*(3), 241–47.
19 Norem, J. (2001). *The positive power of negative thinking.* Cambridge, MA: Basic Books.
20 Babcock, L., Laschever, S., Gelfand M., & Small, D. (2003, October). Nice girls don't ask. *Harvard Business Review.* https://hbr.org/2003/10/nice-girls-dont-ask
21 https://www.marieforleo.com/2011/01/gain-selfconfidence-business/
22 Biswas-Diener, R. (2012). *The courage quotient.* San Francisco: Jossey-Bass.
23 Gilovich, T., & Medvec, V. H. (1995). The experience of regret: What, when, and why. *Psychological Review, 102*(2), 379–95.
24 Damisch, L., Stoberock, B., & Mussweiler, T. (2010). Keep your fingers crossed! How superstition improves performance. *Psychological Science, 21*, 1014–20.
25 Personal interview with Jennifer Crocker via Skype, January 15, 2015. Crocker, J., & Park, L. E. (2004). The costly pursuit of self-esteem. *Psychological Bulletin, 130*, 392–414.
26 Haggbloom, S. J., Warnick, R., Warnick, J. E., Jones, V. K., Yarbrough, G. L., Russell, T. M, ... Monte, E. (2002). The 100 most eminent psychologists of the 20th century. *Review of General Psychology, 6*(2), 139–52.
27 Bandura, Albert. (1997). *Self-efficacy: The exercise of control.* New York: Freeman.
28 Rosenthal, R., & Jacobsen, L. (1968). *Pygmalion in the classroom: Teacher expectation and pupils' intellectual development.* New York: Holt, Rinehart & Winston.
29 Krelman, G., Koch, C., & Fried, I. (2000). Imagery neurons in the human brain. *Nature, 408*, 357–61.
30 Dyson interview. YouTube. https://www.youtube.com/watch?v=I-WRgQlzES8

31 Seligman, M. E. P. (1991). *Learned optimism: How to change your mind and your life.* New York: Knopf.
32 Ericsson, K. A., Krampe, R. Th., & Tesch-Romer, C. (1993). The role of deliberate practice in the acquisition of expert performance. *Psychological Review, 100*, 363–406.
33 Baumeister, R. F., Bratslavsky, E., Finkenauer, C., & Vohs, K. D. (2001). Bad is stronger than good. *Review of General Psychology, 5*(4), 323–70.
34 Dickerson, S. S., & Kemeny, M. E. (2004). Acute stressors and cortisol responses: A theoretical integration and synthesis of laboratory research. *Psychological Bulletin, 130*, 355–91.
35 Neff, K. D. (2011). *Self-compassion.* New York: William Morrow.
36 Neff, K. D., Hseih, Y., & Dejitthirat, K. (2005). Self-compassion, achievement goals, and coping with academic failure. *Self and Identity, 4*, 263–87.
37 Personal interview with Dr. Neff via Skype, February 19, 2015. See also Neff, K. D. (2011). *Self-compassion.* New York: William Morrow.
38 See Marie TV at https://www.youtube.com/user/marieforleo
39 Canfield, J., & Switzer, J. (2005). *The success principles: How to get from where you are to where you want to be.* New York: Harper Resource Book. Here is a great online resource with guidelines for creating a successful mastermind group: https://jackcanfield.com/images/stories/TSP-Mastermind.pdf
40 Driskell, J. E., Copper, C., & Moran, A. (1994). Does mental practice enhance performance? *Journal of Applied Psychology, 79*(4), 481–92.
41 Taylor, S. E., Pham, L. B., Rivkin, I. D., & Armor, D. A. (1998). Harnessing the imagination: Mental simulation, self-regulation, and coping. *American Psychologist, 53*, 429–39.
42 Shantz, A., & Latham, G. (2011). The effect of primed goals on employee performance: Implications for human resource management. *Human Resource Management, 50*(2), 289–99.
43 Kirschenbaum, D. S., Ordman, A. M., Tomarken, A. J., & Holtzbauer, R. (1982). Effects of differential self-monitoring and level of mastery on sports performance: Brain power bowling. *Cognitive Therapy and Research, 6*(3), 335–41.
44 You'll find information about the 2016 ICF Global Coaching Study at http://coachfederation.org/about/landing.cfm?ItemNumber=3936
45 Rosenthal, R., & Jacobson, L. (1968). *Pygmalion in the classroom: Teacher expectation and pupils' intellectual development.* New York: Holt, Rinehart & Winston.
46 Dweck, C. S. (2008). *Mindset: The new psychology of success.* New York: Ballantine Books.
47 Cuddy, A. J. C., Wilmuth, C. A., & Carney, D. R. (2012). The benefit of power posing before a high-stakes social evaluation. Harvard Business School Working Paper No. 13-027.

48 Carney, D. R., Cuddy, A. J., & Yap, A. J. (2015). Review and summary of research on the embodied effects of expansive (vs. contractive) nonverbal displays. *Psychological Science*, *26*(5), 657–63.

49 Nolen-Hoeksema, S., Wisco, B. E., & Lyubomirsky, S. (2008). Re-thinking rumination. *Perspectives on Psychological Science*, *3*(5), 400–24.

50 Fredrickson, B. L. (2009). *Positivity.* New York: Three Rivers Press.

51 Dr. Fredrickson recently came under fire for her work with Marsial Losada and his mathematical conclusions that a 3:1 ratio brings us to a threshold of thriving. Fredrickson returned with a brilliant response in support of her theories on the positivity ratio. Fredrickson, B. L. (2013). Updated thinking on positivity ratios. *American Psychologist*, *68*(9), 814–22.

Bibliography

Arkin, R. M., Oleson, K. C., & Carroll, P. J. (Eds.). (2010). *Handbook of the uncertain self.* New York: Taylor and Francis.

Bandura, A. (1997). *Self-efficacy: The exercise of control.* New York: Freeman.

Baumeister, R. F., Bratslavsky, E., Finkenauer, C., & Vohs, K. D. (2001). Bad is stronger than good. *Review of General Psychology, 5*(4), 323–70.

Berglas, S., & Jones, E. (1978). Drug choice as a self-handicapping strategy in response to non-contingent success. *Journal of Personality and Social Psychology, 36*, 405–17.

Biswas-Diener, R. (2012). *The courage quotient.* San Francisco: Jossey-Bass.

Braslow, M. D., Guerrettaz, J., Arkin, R. M., & Oleson, K. C. (2012). Self-Doubt. *Social and Personality Psychology Compass, 6*, 470–82.

Burns, D. D. (1981). *Feeling good: The new mood therapy.* New York: Penguin Books.

Canfield, J., & Switzer, J. (2005). *The success principles: How to get from where you are to where you want to be.* New York: Harper Resource Book.

Carroll, P. J., Arkin, R. M., & Shade, C. (2011). Possible selves and self-doubt: A poverty of desired possibility. *Journal of Social Psychological and Personality Science*, *2*(2), 190–98.

Clance, P. R., & Imes, S. A. (1978). The impostor phenomenon in high achieving women: Dynamics and therapeutic intervention. *Psychotherapy: Theory, Research & Practice*, *15*(3), 241–47.

Crocker, J., & Park, L. E. (2004). The costly pursuit of self-esteem. *Psychological Bulletin*, *130*, 392–414.

Cuddy, A. J. C., Wilmuth, C. A., & Carney, D. R. (2012). The benefit of power posing before a high-stakes social evaluation. Harvard Business School Working Paper No. 13-027.

Damisch, L., Stoberock, B., & Mussweiler, T. (2010). Keep your fingers crossed! How superstition improves performance. *Psychological Science*, *21*, 1014–20.

Dickerson, S. S., & Kemeny, M. E. (2004). Acute stressors and cortisol responses: A theoretical integration and synthesis of laboratory research. *Psychological Bulletin*, *130*, 355–91.

Driskell, J. E., Copper, C., & Moran, A. (1994). Does mental practice enhance performance? *Journal of Applied Psychology*, *79*(4), 481–92.

Dweck, C. S. (2007). Is math a gift? Beliefs that put females at risk. In S. J. Ceci, & W. M. Williams (Eds.), *Why aren't more women in science? Top researchers debate the evidence* (47–55). Washington, DC: American Psychological Association.

Dweck, C. S. (2008). *Mindset: The new psychology of success.* New York: Ballantine Books.

Eisenberger, N. I., Lieberman, M. D., & Williams, K. D. (2003). Does rejection hurt? An fMRI study of social exclusion. *Science, 302*(5643), 290–92.

Ericsson, K. A., Krampe, R. Th., & Tesch-Romer, C. (1993). The role of deliberate practice in the acquisition of expert performance. *Psychological Review, 100*, 363–406.

Fredrickson, B. L. (2009). *Positivity.* New York: Three Rivers Press.

Fredrickson, B. L. (2013). Updated thinking on positivity ratios. *American Psychologist, 68*(9), 814–22.

Gilovich, T., & Medvec, V. H. (1995). The experience of regret: What, when, and why. *Psychological Review, 102*(2), 379–95.

Haggbloom, S. J., Warnick, R., Warnick, J. E., Jones, V. K., Yarbrough, G. L., Russell, T. M., . . . Monte, E. (2002). The 100 most eminent psychologists of the 20th century. *Review of General Psychology, 6*(2), 139–52.

Hefferon, K. (2013). *The body and positive psychology: The somatopsychic side to flourishing.* London: McGraw-Hill.

Kirschenbaum, D. S., Ordman, A. M., Tomarken, A. J., & Holtzbauer, R. (1982). Effects of differential self-monitoring and level of mastery on sports performance: Brain power bowling. *Cognitive Therapy and Research, 6*(3), 335–41.

Krelman, G., Koch, C., & Fried, I. (2000). Imagery neurons in the human brain. *Nature, 408*, 357–61.

Maddux, J. E. (2002). Self-efficacy: The power of believing you can. In C. R. Snyder & S. J. Lopez (Eds.), *Handbook of positive psychology* (277–87). New York: Oxford University Press.

Mirels, H. L., Greblo, P., & Dean, J. B. (2002). Judgmental self-doubt: Beliefs about one's judgmental prowess. *Personality and Individual Differences, 33*, 741–58.

Neff, K. D. (2011). *Self-compassion.* New York: William Morrow.

Neff, K. D., Hseih, Y., & Dejitthirat, K. (2005). Self-compassion, achievement goals, and coping with academic failure. *Self and Identity*, *4*, 263–87.

Nolen-Hoeksema, S. (1993). *Sex differences in depression.* Stanford, CA: Stanford University Press.

Nolen-Hoeksema, S., Wisco, B. E., & Lyubomirsky, S. (2008). Rethinking rumination. *Perspectives on Psychological Science*, *3*(5), 400–24.

Norem, J. (2001). *The positive power of negative thinking.* Cambridge, MA: Basic Books.

Oleson, K. C., Poehlmann, K. M., Yost, J. H., Lynch, M. E., & Arkin, R. M. (2000). Subjective overachievement: Individual differences in self-doubt and concern with performance. *Journal of Personality*, *68*(3), 491–524.

Pollay, D. J. (2011). *Law of the garbage truck.* New York: Sterling.

Rosenthal, R., & Jacobson, L. (1968). *Pygmalion in the classroom: Teacher expectation and pupils' intellectual development.* New York: Holt, Rinehart & Winston.

Ryan, R. M., & Deci, E. L. (2000). Self-determination theory and the facilitation of intrinsic motivation, social development, and well-being. *American Psychologist*, *55*(1), 68–78.

Sandberg, S. (2013). *Lean in: Women, work, and the will to lead* (1st ed.). New York: Alfred A. Knopf.

Seligman, M. E. P. (1991). *Learned optimism: How to change your mind and your life.* New York: Knopf.

Seligman, M. E. P. (1993). *What you can change and what you can't: The complete guide to successful self-improvement.* New York: Knopf.

Seligman, M. E. P. (2002). *Authentic happiness: Using the new positive psychology to realize your potential for lasting fulfillment.* New York: Free Press.

Seligman, M. E. P. (2011). *Flourish: A visionary new understanding of happiness and well-being.* New York: Free Press.

Shantz, A., & Latham, G. (2011). The effect of primed goals on employee performance: Implications for human resource management. *Human Resource Management*, *50*(2), 289–99.

Sheldon, K. M., & Elliot, A. J. (1999). Goal striving, need satisfaction, and longitudinal well-being: The self-concordance model. *Journal of Personality and Social Psychology*, *76*(3), 482–97.

Stevenson, B., & Wolfers, J. (2009). The paradox of declining female happiness. *American Economic Journal: Economic Policy*, *1*(2), 190–225.

Taylor, S. E., Pham, L. B., Rivkin, I. D., & Armor, D. A. (1998). Harnessing the imagination: Mental simulation, self-regulation, and coping. *American Psychologist*, *53*, 429–39.

About the Author
Louisa Jewell, MAPP

• • • • •

LOUISA IS A speaker, entrepreneur, workshop facilitator, and author who is passionate about empowering women around the world.

Growing up as the fourth child of Sicilian immigrants in Toronto, Louisa learned a certain feistiness to get what she wanted, but she always questioned herself and wondered if she was good enough. After some family tragedies and four miscarriages, Louisa found herself in a deep and dark depression. Determined to take control of her own psychological well-being and happiness, Louisa discovered the amazing study and practice of positive psychology.

In her forties, Louisa returned to school and graduated from the groundbreaking Master of Applied Positive Psychology (MAPP) program at the University of Pennsylvania. The MAPP program is the first master's program in the world to offer in-depth study of the science of happiness and well-being. There, Louisa was taught by the field's founder, renowned psychologist Dr. Martin Seligman. This transformed her life and set her on a new trajectory, and she never found herself in a depression again.

Shortly after completing her master's, Louisa founded the Canadian Positive Psychology Association and served as the founding president for six years (www.cppa.ca). The CPPA brings together leading-edge researchers and practitioners from around the world to study and understand where human potential, success, and happiness intersect. Her hugely successful national conferences draw an international audience of leaders in this field.

Louisa has spoken to thousands of people around the world about how to increase happiness, resilience, and meaning so that people can show up as their best selves and do their best work. She teaches positive psychology at the University of Texas, Dallas, and has taught at the University of Toronto. She regularly delivers webinars and workshops to clients in all sectors.

Her work has been featured in *Forbes*, *Globe and Mail*, *Toronto Star*, *Huffington Post*, *Toronto Sun*, *Canadian Living*, *Live Happy* magazine, *Chatelaine*, *Psychology Today*, and *Women's Agenda*, among other publications. She is a contributing author to *Positive Psychology at Work*, *Positive Psychology News Daily*, and *Psychologie Positive en Environnement professionnel.* She is also a contributing author to the bestselling book *Ready Set Live: Empowering Strategies for an Enlightened Life* and *Character Strengths Matter: How to Live a Full Life.*

Louisa is so proud of her two gorgeous daughters, whom she adores, and still has an excellent friendship with her ex-husband, Tim. When she is not working, she is spending time with her amazing tribe of outstanding women, dancing, doing yoga, trying to do CrossFit, going for nature walks with Sam (her lovable miniature goldendoodle), and making trips to Sicily (her soul's home). She considers herself to be a work in progress and embraces her funny self with love and compassion, flaws and all.

To find out more about Louisa's workshops and to gain inspiration from her blogs and podcasts, visit www.louisajewell.com.

IF YOU HAVE been inspired by this book and want to learn more, Louisa Jewell regularly delivers inspiring and engaging keynote talks, workshops, and webinars across Canada and around the world that educate groups on how to increase positivity, boost confidence, improve well-being, and unlock optimal performance.

Visit www.louisajewell.com and sign up for Louisa's newsletter to find out about opportunities to participate in her public workshops, weekly podcasts, and online learning programs.

We would love to hear about your stories of confidence and success in your life, so stay in touch!

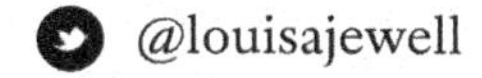

www.facebook.com/louisajewellflourishwithconfidence

CPSIA information can be obtained
at www.ICGtesting.com
Printed in the USA
BVOW08s1936100917
494494BV00001B/60/P